from Debi –
Christmas 1998

# Ginny's Chairs

by

Virginia Wing Power

**BookTree Press**
A Division of Phase II: Publications
Chattanooga, Tennessee

Printed in the United States of America.

First edition published in 1998.

Library of Congress Catalog Card Number 98-70593

Power, Virginia Wing
Ginny's Chairs: a biographical collection of
stories, insights and poems from a remarkable
Southern lady whose lifetime spanned most
of the twentieth century.

ISBN 0-9644760-6-1. $25.00

Nancy Franklin Hartung was principal editor, researcher, and
writing assistant to Mrs. Power.
Stella H. Dunlap provided years of invaluable assistance with
the compilation of materials for the book.
Linda L. Burton, Phase II: Publications, provided editing and
book production services.
Connie Roberts, Connie Roberts Communications, designed
the book jacket.
Thomson-Shore book manufacturers of Dexter, Michigan
printed the book.

To order please contact:
Phase II: Publications                 or the
5251-C Hwy 153, #255                    Virginia Wing Power Estate
Chattanooga, TN 37343                   PO Box 669
T 423-876-8456 F 423-876-8457           Chattanooga, TN 37401

# Comments

*"Ginny Power combines all of the charm of the traditional Southern Belle with all of the drive of a Scarlett O'Hara, but without Scarlett's less desirable characteristics." Dorothy Patten "Love of Chattanooga" Award*

*"Ginny Power's motto is 'To do and not to be done for,'" Kiwanis Award Presentation speech by Gordon Fitzell*

*"Ginny is of the opinion that 'to make good old people, you have to catch them young.'" Junior League Jottings*

*"Ginny Power never found the time to become a full-fledged senior citizen. She was too busy looking after others." Chattanooga Times*

*"Ginny Power's life and times are a story worth telling." Chattanooga Free Press*

*"Ginny... enjoyed using the military term 'pass muster.' Living life the way Ginny did for 91 years is the epitome of 'passing muster,' it seems to me." Nancy Franklin Hartung*

*"Ginny was in my acting class for 18 years. Plays that she wrote always showed her amazing insight, compassion, and knowledge of relationships, which is what theatre is all about." Nancy Lane Wright*

*"She had nearly a century of firsthand knowledge about love...and laughter. If I could pattern my life after one person, I would choose Mrs. Ginny. She taught me a new meaning of caring." Leisa Lewis, LPN*

*"Ginny Power inspired people, kept them going and propelled them in directions that resulted in action...she turned old age into victory...adding life to years she added years to life."*

# Ginnyisms

*"As you grow older, your world expands instead of getting smaller. I have watched things grow beyond my dreams and I have stayed around and participated in them."*

*"Start with what you have and work from there. You've got to feel you have forever to do it."*

*"Life is like a garden. It is never static."*

*"I'm a real dirt gardener. I have a beautiful garden, and I'm just a plain dirt gardener who loves it."*

*"The things you do in later life you do partly because you want to, but I've found that they pay such dividends, it's the serendipity in life."*

*"To everything there is a season... if you open your eyes to the opportunities."*

*"People are younger at older ages these days."*

*"You can't keep a muscle young but you can certainly keep it going."*

*Playing tennis in the Tennessee Senior Olympics at age 79, Ginny battled 96-degree temperatures and a 55-and-up age category to win a gold and bronze medal. "It was fun," she said. "But the volunteer rescue squad sat alongside the courts as we played!"*

*Ginny was instrumental in having a questionnaire sent to nearly 3,000 elderly people in the 1950's, and the conclusion called for action. At the newly forming group's second meeting, someone asked her "What are you going to do to entertain us?" "Nothing!" was the answer. "There are refreshments to be fixed and served, now come on, let's all get busy."*

# Table of Contents

# Table of Contents

# Virginia Wing Power
## 1906 – 1997

# The Universal Mind

I made a bowl of biscuits,
Rolled them and cut them out
Each one alike.
In the oven they baked and browned.
But they were not alike, no two,
Even though they were of the same stuff.

My fat nephew took the biggest.
I was glad they left the brownest for me.
As hostess, I couldn't choose,
But like my biscuits brown.

They were the same stuff,
All biscuits. Nobody said,
What is this strange thing?

Then, in the small night, not sleeping,
(maybe from too many biscuits)
Sitting in Auntie's gooseneck rocker,
With a lonely light,
A thought came, an idea,
So new, but simple, workable.

Why had no one thought this way before?
Hundreds would know, millions,
That since all time, this thing, this hidden thing,
Had rested, waiting to be found,
To smooth brows, solve puzzlements,
And push fear back.

Excited then, and not knowing or caring,
How an old woman in curl rollers
Might think new thoughts,
But knowing I must sleep,
I read John Donne.
Read for solace, for forgetfulness,
For tempting sleep.

But Donne was tempting God,
Was flashing ideas,
And crashing words against each other.
Hunting, always hunting, for the unexplained.

He dipped into the bowl of secret knowledge,
As I had dipped,
As savages and Greeks have done,
Baking ideas as any man can bake them
(Or half bake them).

We all may dip, and do,
And nothing we find, or everything, is new.

*Virginia Wing Power*

# Virginia Wing Power

Virginia "Ginny" Wing Power, a longtime Chattanoogan, was born, grew up, and married in historic Bulloch Hall in Roswell, Georgia. Ginny went to school at North Avenue Presbyterian School in Atlanta (now the Westminster Schools) and received her B. A. from Agnes Scott College in Decatur, Georgia. She was a feature writer for the *Atlanta Georgian* newspaper before marrying George W. Power and moving to Chattanooga in 1928.

When George entered the Army early in World War II, Ginny joined the American Red Cross and found herself not far from the front lines at a field hospital. The experience changed her understanding of what one person can accomplish. Having no children of her own, she took the world and its needs to heart.

After the war she did volunteer work through Junior League marionette shows, children's theater, and dramatic radio programs. Ginny was active in the YWCA, Health Department, Family Service Agency, St Paul's Episcopal Church, Reflection Riding, Department of Human Services, and the Junior League.

She was co-founder and first president of Senior Neighbors of Chattanooga, Inc., and served on the founding committee of St. Barnabas Retirement Complex.

Ginny received numerous awards for service including the Kiwanis Distinguished Service Award, the Business Women's A to Z Award, the Dorothy Patten "Love of Chattanooga" Award, Outstanding Alumnae Award of Agnes Scott College, and citations from the American Association of Retired Persons and local and state governments.

Ginny also was well known for the two-acre garden in Riverview she landscaped and designed. For its creation she pored over gardening books, walked the finest gardens in the United States and abroad, and planted with hands-on intensity. For many years it has been open to the public each spring.

Full of friendliness, fun and frivolity, she enjoyed wilderness hiking and horseback pack trips, fly fishing, teaching exercise classes, writing and acting in plays, and tennis. She was a charter member of the Chattanooga Tennis Club and was a tennis gold medalist at the National Senior Games at age 87.

## Reach

Get on with you.
You've got no time for
 that.
There's a sunset outside
And dinner to make.
A hungry dog and cat, too,
They would dislike your
 finishing life.
And for now, you might
 just get back
To straightening up those
 files
That have been cluttering
The workroom for weeks.
When Life is through with
 you, it will
Let you know, or maybe it
 won't.
The woman you have
 made wears
Many faces. Underneath
 somewhere
Is a dewy twenties child.
And if you can't carve the
 smile
In outside wood to look at,
Toss it around inside and
 glad to do it.

ॐ

Ginny Power's life spanned most of the twentieth century. Throughout her 91-year lifetime she loved people, and loved bringing out the best in them. She wanted to see them stand tall in their own self-respect.

Ginny died at home, near her beloved garden, on November 23, 1997. Earlier in the week she and her gardener discussed the placement of four thousand new tulip bulbs, twice as many as usual, as preparations were made for spring.

Her dining room table was stacked with poetry, photographs, and several versions of her manuscript as she put the finishing touches on this compilation of life vignettes. She tells her stories as honestly as a loved and loving child would tell them, painting images to share, showing the growth of a strong and independent woman.

Step back to another time and place and follow Ginny through the twentieth century. Look at every photograph; see her view of life through her shining smile. Her poetry allows the most personal glimpse of all; straight from her heart, it will surely wrap itself around yours. Please take a seat in one of Ginny's chairs; we join her on the porch of Bulloch Hall. It is 1907.

# Bulloch Hall

Bulloch Hall stands gracefully atop a hill at the end of Roswell's Bulloch Avenue, only 20 miles from downtown Atlanta. Some distance from the main highway, it is enveloped in a grove of forest oaks.

The imposing white clapboard house of heart-pine was designed for Major James S. Bulloch, his wife Martha, and their six children. Major Bulloch was the maternal grandfather of Theodore Roosevelt, Jr., 26th President of the United States.

The hand-sawn lumber, after seasoning for a year or more, was put together with wooden pegs. The four massive Doric columns were built by slave carpenters, and the bricks were handmade of clay from the nearby Chattahoochee River.

Built in 1840, it was modeled on the plan of the ancient Parthenon at Athens, and has been preserved exactly as originally built—magnificently sound and solidly serene.

A day of major significance in the mansion's history was December 22, 1853, when Martha "Mittie" Bulloch and Theodore Roosevelt were married there, "an occasion marked by unusual splendor."

The historic Georgia landmark survived the onslaught of Union troops who visited the area 13 times. It was Union Army headquarters as they prepared for the attack on Atlanta.

Margaret Mitchell is believed to have derived some of her images for Tara from her many visits to the house.

Major Bulloch died after living in his beloved Bulloch Hall less than ten years. Ownership changed numerous times after that, but the Wood family owned Bulloch Hall in the late 1800's and the Wing family from the early 1900's until 1971.

In 1974 the City of Roswell, with assistance from the Georgia Department of Natural Resources, passed a bond referendum and purchased Bulloch Hall and the surrounding sixteen acres. It is now open to the public and features a Bulloch-Roosevelt Room and a Wood-Wing Room.

## A Villanelle, 1974

Dear, fine place, dear house where I was born,
Who knows you now, who loves that high, cool room?
Must I always miss you, forever be forlorn?
I have a garden here. It lures me every morn.
But there's a need, deeper than for bloom,
That calls me there, house where I was born.
Three-sashed windows, so tall a world they show,
Bright, child's world, marred by no trace of gloom,
Must I always miss you, forever be forlorn?
I feared no ghosts. For there they gently go
And bring no hurt nor any sense of doom
In that dear place, old house where I was born.
Rain on my roof, could I that fresh sleep know,
And clear young trust for which no dangers loom?
Must I always miss you, forever be forlorn?
"Come back, come home."
Plain as any horn it sounds. I hear and know for whom.
Dear lost place, dear house where I was born,
Must I always miss you, sometimes feel forlorn?

# Ghosts of Bulloch Hall

Of course there are ghosts at Bulloch Hall.
I know, because I am one.
Here, scramble up the mimosa tree,
There by the corner of the porch steps.
Settle into the crotch of limbs.
Watch. Be very quiet.

## The Steps at the Back of the Porch

A girl appears wearing blue crepe de chine,
And carrying two glasses of tea, clinking
With ice-wagon ice. She sits on the corner
Of one of the tall, while columns, jiggling
The tea to cool it. She looks about twelve
And has dancing eyes.
A slim woman comes out of the wide front door.
"I do think John Coolie tried himself
On his tomatoes this year. Now, wasn't it
Worth it, spending half an hour making mayonnaise?
Always use very thin, freshly sliced
Homemade bread. You won't forget
When you are grown?"
Pistachio Columbine Mimosa,
The girl's white cat, walks up,
Carrying her tail high, with only a slight,
A tiny crook at the end. "Tashy, darling,
Would you like a bit of tomato sandwich?"
Tashy wouldn't.

You can come down now from your perch
In the tree. They have vanished,
They are gone. It's a way ghosts have.
The steps are empty. The breeze
From the beech tree sweeps across.
And somewhere a cardinal
Sings his summer mating song.

## The Upstairs Landing

The chief place for ghosts at Bulloch Hall
Is the upstairs stairway landing.
You can feel them there,
Know they are about. Here, climb out
Onto the tin roof above the kitchen.
Look in through the hall window.
Stay silent, no matter what.
There it is! Do you see it?
Covered by transparent, floaty,
Fly-away things. Creeping down the stairs.

"Oh no...you shouldn't. Why are you here?"
From the shadows, a voice, a man's voice:
"Do you know how beautiful you are,
Floating with the moon?"
"Oh..." A long sigh.
"I've never been kissed
In my nightie before. It's scary. Sort of.
What was that noise? Someone's awake.
Please go. Hurry."

Two doors close
On opposite sides of the hall.
The lace curtains stir at the window
Making flickering patterns on the empty stairs.

## The Parlor

It's no matter. She is sobbing so
She'll never hear you. That is,
If ghosts can hear. Just stand there
Behind the portiere at the folding doors
And you can safely watch.
Shades at the high windows are drawn
Against late summer heat.

She holds a red book with a gold flower
Etched into the cover.
The hall door opens.
"Have you found a good book, dear?"
"One of the French books
I brought home from school,
Pierre Loti's Madame Chrysantheme."
"I hope you are enjoying it."

The door closes. From beneath
The tapestry pillow at her head,
The girl takes out a photograph.
She gazes into lively eyes beneath
Slick, stuck-down nineteen-twenties hair.

"It is the end," she whispers to the picture.
"Chrysantheme will never see her lover again,
And I won't see you. Not in a thousand years.
Are you missing me at all? Or have you found
Already, some stylish, sophisticated Yankee girl?"
Again she dissolves into sobs and floods
Of tears. Then she is gone. Vanished.
The room is empty, lonely and quiet,
Except for a few sobs that hang,
Perhaps forever, on the still, cool air.

## The Dining Room

Folding doors to the parlor stand
Wide open. The rooms are filled
With chattering, ghostly guests.
Slip quietly in and join them,
You won't be noticed in the crowd.

Mrs. Jackson, the old music teacher,
Is playing a Debussy piece. That girl!
Why would she choose these strange chords
Telling of a church that rises from the sea
After a hundred years? Is that wedding music?
There. On the stairway. She is coming
On her tall brother's arm, rustling
In stiff, creamy satin and duchesse lace.
Dr. Flinn edges round an altar palm,
Smiling reassurance. But for her,
A moment's panic: He looks so serious.
He slips the ring upon her finger
Carefully, as Dr. Flinn had taught them.
"Because some people are a little nervous
At this time." She feels his strong, warm hand,
Holding her cold one safe.

There is prohibition punch with wedding cake.
"A beautiful wedding, wasn't it? Simple
But beautiful. Such a lovely bride."
(Guest talk). "She isn't really wearing white,
Is she? The cream color is becoming.
But of course most brides choose white,
So virginal."

Then it's over and they come running
Down the stairs, dressed for motoring.
Zing. Zing. Rice bounces off the Ford coupe,
The new-fangled self-starter works
The first time. And they are off.

Inside the house, the grandfather clock
Begins to strike, goes on a striking spree.
You count to sixty, then lose count.
Is it striking years ahead? Or is it,
In fact, cathedral bells we hear ringing across
A new and untried sea?

They have gone now. All the ghosts are gone,
The bride's mother enters the empty house,
Bends to smell a tea rose,
But already the petals are falling,
Drifting gently through sun-streaked air.

# Hattie and Bartow

Hattie was a proper Victorian lady. After her father's death, she dutifully stayed with Mama until her younger sister was old enough to take over. Then, for a couple of years, she was daring indeed, teaching in Tampa, Florida, learning to eat Cuban food, and sometimes wearing a bathing costume to the beach.

Hattie was my mother, and it is my good fortune that when she was twenty-eight years old (not that she would have admitted being that old), she finally found her man.

The odor of food being prepared drifted up the stairs to her room where she was reading. She was not domestically inclined, and the purpose of her present visit to her sister Boyce's home was to rest and recuperate after typhoid fever. She was one of the lucky ones who had the fever and lived. But there was no possibility of going back to Florida to teach this year. She heard her sister's voice at the foot of the stairs calling her.

"Hattie, supper's ready."

She came to the head of the stairs. "Do I have to? I'm in the most interesting place in my book."

"Of course, you have to. You are supposed to eat a lot. And you've read that book at least sixteen times."

Hattie often thought afterwards how narrowly she missed seeing him. She brought her bedroom lamp downstairs and set it on the hall table, ready to light her way back upstairs after supper. She had been reading about Sir Kenneth, the Scottish Crusader, and his noble hound, Roswal. Even the dogs in Sir Walter Scott's novels were noble creatures.

As she came into the dining room, a man seated next to her vacant place at the table rose to his feet.

"Hattie, this is Mr. Wing from Roswell. He is here on a lumber-buying trip, and is spending the night with us. Mr. Wing, this is my sister, Hattie."

"From Roswell," she murmured. "Strange, I've just been reading in Sir Walter Scott's novel, *The Talisman* about Roswal, the noble hound. Do you know the book?"

"No," he said. "I've been too busy to do much reading. And I don't see to read at night."

"My sister says I have read *The Talisman* sixteen times. I wish I could make you a gift of one of my readings. It is such a thrilling book."

"I wish you could do that, Miss Hattie," he said. "There is a great deal I have missed in life."

After that, Brother Max took over the conversation, talking man-talk with the guest. It was just before the meal was finished that the shock hit her. She had split a hot biscuit and poured cream gravy over it from the gravy boat.

"Would you like some gravy, Mr. Wing?" she asked politely.

"Thank you, it is delicious," he said.

As she passed the dish to him, their hands touched. He told her, long afterward, that a bowl of gravy had been his downfall. Perhaps it was for both. For from that moment, others around the table faded from their consciousness.

After supper Max excused himself to look after a sick horse in the barn, and Boyce took the children to bed.

"Don't go," he begged Hattie when she prepared to say good night. "You owe me a reading. Would you bring your book and read me something from it?"

She read until the oil in her lamp burned low, and the lamp began to smoke. Then she lowered the flame, and they talked of really important things. That he had never been married and neither had she; that he owned a big house, and his sister and her family made a home for him there. Green eyes, he told her, were his idea of just the right color to set off a beautiful face.

When he said that, she burst out. "With this awful, short hair!" she wailed. "It all came out when I had the fever."

"Let's set our wedding date soon, before your hair grows long," he said. "Because if you looked any prettier, I don't think I could stand it."

Hattie grabbed the lamp and ran up the stairs, almost dropping it in her confusion. But at the head of the stairs she turned and gave him a very small smile.

"I mean it," he said. And he did.

They were married on December 14, 1904, three

days before Hattie's twenty-ninth birthday. The date represented careful planning on Hattie's part. It would give her hair time to grow, yet at age twenty-eight, she would still be comfortably in her twenties, not quite an old maid.

Bartow took her to live in Bulloch Hall, one of the beautiful antebellum homes built in the small village of Roswell, Georgia, during the 1840's. I, the Wing's first child, was born there on Good Friday, April 13, 1906. It was a long, uneasy birth, a breech presentation. Hattie remembered that between whiffs of chloroform, she overhead the doctor say to his assisting nurse, "I think we can save the mother, but I am not sure about the baby."

The double miracle did occur. Bartow was invited in to see his wife and new daughter. Lying in the big double bed that had been moved into the downstairs sitting room for the occasion, Hattie wore the inimitable look of a new mother's sublime achievement, while I must have appeared somewhat battered.

"I think, in a few days when the redness clears up," Hattie said tentatively, "she may be real pretty."

"In a few days," my father thundered. "Why, she is perfectly beautiful right now!"

# Satirists Are Born

There is no bitterness in my heart.
How should there be?

A childhood that brought joy wrapped in love,
Set against hills and pastures,
Roamed with Father who knew all trees,
And understood what children imagined
From a poplar whistle at spring when it slipped,
And you could call up fairies with it
To an argosy of rusted farm wagons
That were airplane carriers complete
With landing decks, doctors and nurses
In high-button shoes and Red Cross headbands.

And a mother better not to describe
Because she was love incarnate
And wrapped us in understanding and stimulus.
And she was beauty.

The rest of life, the living part?
If I should try forever,
Or for that forever which is left,
A few, too few, years.
I could not say thank you to the world,
Nor to my strong man,
Nor to the fall of the dice,
Or more to my belief, the plan of God,
That has made my days one long opportunity.

# Clearly a Place for Chairs

My lifetime has spanned most of a century. It was a world that can never come again. There were many Southern families much like ours. And yet, our kind of people aren't truly known nor historically recognized.

We were not decadent, and we would not have made characters for Poe's stories. We lacked shock value. Yet the whirlpool of twentieth century turbulence sucked us in. So far, I have never quite lost that battered look, but I have survived.

"She sho' ain't no lady that loves a bed," I heard my new household assistant telling a telephone friend.

She was talking about me, and already she knew. Action is my dish. Thus, it seems even to me a little out of character that I find myself now thinking about chairs I have known.

This rather compulsive search in the dusty closet of the past began late on a night when I was enjoying a visit from a newish sort of friend, insomnia. Sleeplessness may shorten life, but for me, it adds a lot of pleasure, giving me bonus time for reading and thinking during hours when things are quiet.

On one sleepless night I got up and barefooted my way toward my dressing room in the dark so as not to waken my sleeping husband. I felt for the back of the slim, ladderback chair I used as a guide. Touching the smooth top rung of that chair is in itself a thrill.

Often I can see my mother sitting in that chair before her bedroom desk in my childhood home. I see her there, slim neck bent, warm brown hair escaping pins to highlight her cheek, her voice soft, if a little exasperated. "Wait just a minute, dear, Mother's *adding*."

I went past the desk into my dressing room and switched on the light, found my book, and settled down in Auntie's little gooseneck rocker. But I did not read.

My mind wandered back a hundred years to the time when some unknown workman had shaped this dainty chair for a succession of small women he would never know; then to the time Mother told how Auntie had given it to her, her favorite niece.

"Hattie, it is a perfect chair to bathe babies from, such nice low arms. And to rock them, too. With yours coming along, I want you to have it now."

And I thought how it passed to me, one of the babies bathed from it. What would that long-ago craftsman have thought had he known an old woman would one day be sitting in his chair at two o'clock in the morning, reading by a brilliant light? And that from time to time she took a few sitting-up exercises on the floor while the noise of a passing jet momentarily engulfed the world?

I looked across the dressing room and found myself admiring another chair I had loved from the days it stood silhouetted against the high, white wall of our old front hall, much too small for the space. Because it looked so small against the wide sweep of plaster, it had seemed to me a jewel of a chair. Its legs sweetly curved into its smooth mahogany seat; the back was not tall but made a generous flat frame for the central fiddleback panel, which was the heart of my love.

Sometimes I would sit for all of a minute in that chair, my perspiring short legs doing the varnish no good, but my five-year-old mind enchanted with the feel of it and the coolness of the still hall. The fragrance of the Duchess roses on the big oval table caught my memory, and I could see Daddy's derby hanging on one of the corner hooks of the mirror above. Were hatracks, as Mother said, really going out of style?

# Big Fingerprint

I settled back comfortably into the curve of the gooseneck rocker and began to search, really search my mind for the very first chair I could remember. It was waiting. A big dining room chair for a very little girl.

My father and Nelson had finished unpacking all the chairs. Mother had remarked, "Bartow, I hope the next time Captain Randall comes home with you for dinner and leans back to start telling stories, he can do it without having his chair collapse under him. Of course he must weigh two hundred and fifty. But I was never so embarrassed in my life. Oh, Bartow, look, this one was damaged in shipping, and there is a big rubbed place on the varnish. I suppose we must send it back. Oh dear."

A small girl's arms flew around as much as she could reach of the big chair. "Mother, please don't send it back. It's got a big fingerprint. Baby Tow can have the high chair now. I'm going to sit in the chair with the big fingerprint forever and ever."

"Keep it," my father said with finality. "It's a small price to pay to get her out of that high chair. Every time she climbs in or out I expect catastrophe."

So Big Fingerprint stayed. Catastrophe was not, however, entirely averted. Perched upon two tightly stuffed pillows from the front hall couch, an eager young trencher-person was able to dispatch a meal in something like half the time needed by talkative grownups.

Inevitably there came the meal when the prescribed "May I be excused, please, Mother?" was followed by a barrage of flying pillows as little Virginia disappeared underneath the floor-length white linen tablecloth. The moment of expectant silence dragged out. No screams were heard.

Could she have hit her head and be lying senseless?

"Virginia, Baby, are you all right?"

"Mother, I am down here playing with Boolard."

"Boolard? Who is Boolard?"

"Oh, Mother, Boolard is a boy. He is my friend. This is where he lives."

For the next few days meals ended with little Virginia, and presumably Boolard, crawling under the table and over adult feet.

Daddy was heard to say at intervals, "I only wish she had stayed in the high chair."

Then one day Virginia announced, "Boolard is gone. He doesn't live here now."

As time passed, one of the big sofa cushions was removed, then both. I sat in a bare chair like the grownups. But there was no doubt about priorities with Big Fingerprint.

# The Barrel Chair

Mother never believed in spanking. Not even when I strained the milk and butter through Howard Cosby's big felt hat while he was washing dining room windows.

Not even when she looked at me in horror and said, "Virginia Wing, what do you think I ought to do to you for this?"

Not even when my answer was, "Well, Mother, I think you ought to give me a good spanking."

Mother had read an article in the *Ladies' Home Journal* which said that requiring a naughty child to sit still in a chair was a good method for impressing the enormity of crime upon the young.

The chair she selected was no doubt chosen with great care. It sat in a nook formed by one of the fluted columns that supported an arch separating our front and back halls. It was called a barrel chair, and except for an aperture in front through which the sitter inserted himself, it was indeed almost round. It in no way resembled a barrel except in shape, being made with handsomely turned spindles of a deep black color fashionably known as ebony. It was extremely sturdy, difficult to overturn, and remote from any tables loaded with tempting bric-a-brac.

After some heinous offense I probably should

remember with repentance, I was told to sit in the chair until Mother came for me.

Placing feet in the center of the chair seat and inching myself around in circles was good for a short spell of entertainment. But just as I despaired of time ever passing, I heard the patter of little feet. I looked up with joy to see my brother's fox terrier puppy coming down the hall.

Daddy thought a boy's dog ought to be allowed indoors with his master. Mother thought Tow's puppy would ruin her lovely rugs. So the back porch was Buster's world.

"Buster, you are a bad puppy. Go back."

Any word was a kind word to Buster. He pranced toward me, intent on greeting an old friend.

En route he thought to pause, however. Selecting a lovely red and blue spot on the hall Axminster, he produced a sizeable puddle. This, as I well knew, was the height of enormity.

"Buster!" I yelled, "You bad, bad puppy. Come here this instant. You have to sit in this chair until you can learn to be good."

I made a dive for Buster. He withdrew just beyond reach. The code forbade me to get out of the chair.

The game got better, with Buster approaching, me diving, and Buster always out of reach.

Finally I hooked a foot through the rungs of the chair back and called ever so sweetly, "Nice puppy, good doggie. Come here Buster."

As he approached I launched into a swan dive. My foot held. The resulting crash mingled with child and puppy yelps brought the entire household running.

Looking back, it seems to me that Mother somewhat lost faith in the *Ladies' Home Journal* after that.

Years later as I decided what to keep and what to sell before closing Bulloch Hall, the dealer and I came upon the barrel chair. It was battered but still whole.

No doubt it affirmed the dealer's opinion that old ladies are crazy when I waved vaguely toward that chair and said, "You may as well take this one. It's really too late now for mayhem."

# Baby Bentwood

The mournful sound of the horn went on and on. I had been a good girl and had gone to bed early so Santa Claus could come. The gas was turned low in the chandelier. I could see Tow asleep in his brass youth bed.

But I couldn't go to sleep. All I could hear was the sound of that horn, way off somewhere. Maybe since I was six years old now, Christmas wasn't going to be fun anymore. Maybe Santa Claus couldn't find our house.

The next thing I knew, I felt Mother's arms hugging me. "Merry Christmas, darling. Wake up and let's go see what Santa Claus brought."

I clung to her. "Mother, I dreamed he didn't come. And a horn was blowing."

"You get up and see," said Mother cheerfully.

Tow was already up. He was supposed to be washing his face, but was just scrabbling the water like he always did when Mother was not watching. We put our bathrobes over our Dr. Denton sleepers and Mother led us from the bedroom to the sitting room door.

"Everybody ready? *Open Sesame!*," she sang out as she threw open the door.

The first thing I saw was the big Christmas tree

reaching to the ceiling. All the candles were lighted and flickering on the tinsel and shining ornaments. White tissue-paper-wrapped packages were piled underneath, and hanging from the branches. I saw a drum and some fireworks. Sparklers, I hoped.

Then I looked at the fireplace. Daddy was on his knees in front of it, making the flames leap up the chimney. I saw Tow's stockings bulging with exciting lumps. Beneath them sat a little red wagon full of toys.

My stockings, hanging against the white-fluted columns that I especially loved in that room, were full of lumps and knots too. I could see a candy cane and two Roman candles sticking out the top. On the floor were a doll buggy and two books and a tea set.

And then I saw it.

Around the corner of the mantel, pushed almost out of sight, was the most beautiful little rocking chair in the whole world. I had seen big ones like this. They called them "Bentwood." But this one was little, just right for me.

And sitting in my new chair was the most beautiful doll I'd ever seen. For a moment I couldn't touch her; she was too wonderful. She had dark brown real hair, hanging in ringlets. Her dress was bright pink trimmed with brown velvet bands, and she wore a flower-trimmed velvet hat.

"Do you like her?" Mother asked. "I think Santa Claus brought her to you especially because she has brown eyes, and you have brown eyes, too."

"Her name is Margaret," I said. Then I picked

Margaret up and sat down in the little Bentwood rocker, cradling my new daughter. With a slight clicking sound, Margaret closed her brown eyes, and I saw beautiful, curled lashes against her warm pink cheeks. I began to rock.

After a while Mother said, "Dear, aren't you going to look at the other things Santa brought?"

I didn't answer, I just kept rocking in a symphony of joy.

Mother later said she thought I'd have kept rocking my new doll all day if we had not been interrupted. But the front hall door flew open with a chorus of "Christmas Gift, Christmas Gift, Christmas Gift, Miss Hattie, Christmas Gift, Mr. Bartow."

We saw Bessie Jackson, our cook, her big brother John, and our friend, her little brother Robert.

"Merry Christmas to you all," Daddy said, reaching into his pockets. "You really caught us with 'Christmas Gift' this time."

He handed Bessie and John paper money, then gave Tow and me a quarter each. We knew what to do with the quarters. "Robert," I said, "Merry Christmas. You can buy a lot of penny candy with this."

Mother was handing out wrapped presents. I got Margaret. "Do you like my new doll, Robert?"

Robert did not say much, but Mother stepped into the breach.

"Now," she said, "I believe Santa Claus remembered somebody else around here."

We followed her into the kitchen. Hanging on the kitchen mantel were stockings just like ours with the same interesting bulges. And on the hearth beneath sat a little red wagon.

"Santa Claus brought it to you, Robert," Mother said.

Robert began to cry. Crying, he pulled his wagon around the kitchen, singing a little tune under his breath. I finally made out the words. He was singing, "Thankee, Lord Jesus; thankee, Lord Jesus."

"Robert," I said a bit priggishly, "Lord Jesus didn't bring your wagon, Santa Claus did."

"Are there any difference?" he stopped to say.

There may have been two happier children that Christmas than Robert Jackson and me, but I doubt it.

# He' Ghostie

Tow and I were sitting on our back hall stair steps listening to John Jackson tell about the ghost. John would sometimes come to our house in the evenings to walk home with Bessie and keep the buggers away. Daddy said it was strange the buggers were most dangerous on nights when we had country ham for supper.

"That shows me John is very sensible," Mother said. "Good as your specially cured ham is, John knows he will get some with hominy and ham gravy to go along. He can probably smell that ham cooking all the way to their house."

"That's impossible, Hattie," Daddy said. "It's half a mile to the creek, then clear past Volley Coleman's farm to their house. Nobody can smell ham that far. John must be gifted with telepathy."

I believed John was gifted with very unusual qualities. He knew some strange things.

"John, is there really a ghost in Bulloch Hall?"

"For sure, Missy. Dey done found Ol' Major dead in he' pew at church. Now he' ghostie guardin' he' money right hyah."

John's family had come from the low country, and there was a lot of Geechee in his talk.

"John, does the Major's ghost live in our house all the time?"

"For sure he' ghostie stay 'round hyah. Ain't goin' for to leave he' money."

"Where does the ghost live?"

"Live in attic, maybe in walls; live where be he' money."

It was dim and shadowy on the back steps; chilly there too, for it was early November. In those days, none of the stair halls had lights or heat. I was pretty sure I heard a noise at the head of the steps, a sort of "thump...thump...thump."

"Did you hear that? There is nobody upstairs. Is it the ghost, John?"

"Don't know what sound he make. Mought be he' ghostie."

"Well, I'm glad the door at the head of the stairs is closed." I shivered slightly.

"'Twon't do no good, Missy. He' ghostie don't open doors. He pass through."

Tow spoke up. "I don't believe in ghosts," he said. "And Daddy doesn't either. Tell us about Brer' Rabbit and Brer' Fox, John."

When I told Mother what John said, she was provoked and said he had no business frightening us with ghost stories.

"But he believes in He' Ghostie, Mother."

"Oh, darling, all the old people thought there

was a ghost in this house, but we have lived here all these years and nobody has ever heard or seen one. The story got started because people kept looking for Major Bulloch's money. Old Mrs. Wood told me that when they came here to live, all the hearths had been taken up and holes dug everywhere under the house. Probably there never was any buried money at all. At any rate, none was ever found."

"But Mother, I really did hear a noise. It went 'thump...thump...thump' like it was upstairs."

"Well, darling, if we ever hear the noise again, we will hunt for the source. Now you just forget it."

We did hear the noise again, a few nights later.

"That's it!" I said. "That's He' Ghostie. I'm scared!"

"Nonsense," my father said. "In this old house it's probably the wind creaking or the timbers settling. I'll take a lantern and go see what it is."

By the time Daddy filled the lantern with kerosene, the noise had stopped. He went upstairs anyway. We could hear him walking around.

When he came back downstairs he said, "There is not a thing in the world up there. I went into every room and closet and even looked in the attic."

We continued hearing the noise from time to time, however. Nothing happened, but I was becoming more and more frightened.

Finally one night Daddy said, "All right, we are going on a ghost hunt. Come on everyone, especially you, Virginia."

Daddy lit the lantern and took my hand. "The best way to meet an unknown fear is to find out what it is," he told me.

We went up the front stairs. I dreaded getting to the landing where the back stairs joined because I had a sneaking suspicion He' Ghostie was lurking there.

We got to the landing, went up the broad upper stairs, through the upstairs hall, and into all the bedrooms and closets. Nothing. Then we heard the noise again. It was coming from the attic above us.

"Let's go to the attic," Daddy said. I thought I'd faint, but it had to be done.

Up the narrow, dusty attic stairs our little procession went, with me clinging to Daddy's hand and Mother and Tow behind us. By the dim lantern light I began to recognize things I knew well from playing there. There were the stairs to the tin backporch roof, where you could see the river. I saw the flower-decorated tin bathtubs with seats, used when slaves emptied and filled them. I saw my wicker baby carriage. Daddy led us past piles of magazines and dusty old trunks.

"You see, daughter, there is nothing to be afraid of here," he began. Then there was an awful flapping sound and something nearly knocked me down.

"It's a bird!" my father shouted.

And bird it was. A very interesting bird, indeed. It was a huge woodpecker with only one leg. It had pecked a hole in the corner of the eaves and sought sanctuary in our attic.

Our one-legged woodpecker came back each winter for several years. We learned to know the sound of his half walk, half flop. I was secretly glad to have him there. If He' Ghostie decided to get active, I knew our friend the woodpecker was around to protect us.

# Three Chairs for the Red, White, and Blue

The next chairs that impressed me for life were ushered in on a song. And like a good many deeply memorable adjuncts of life, they never existed at all.

I heard the music waxing strong from my place on the aisle. The chapel bench for my fourth grade class was on the front row. The little first graders were on the front row too. First, second, and third graders sat on one side and fourth, fifth, and sixth sat across from them.

As the youngest and smallest fourth grader, I had the aisle seat.

The first graders were singing and bouncing with such joy that the round collars of their dusty, faded cotton aprons fluttered.

Mother said it was pathetic about the little mill children. Their mothers picked them up out of the yard, put drawers on them, and sent them to school so somebody would look after them. They couldn't be over four years old, some of them.

They used words like "ain't" that I must never use. But I was never to make fun of the mill children. Never. I was to listen and be careful of my own diction.

I did listen. And I noticed they called chairs "cheers" and they said "skeered" instead of saying scared.

I noticed their diction in the new song Mrs. Foster taught us. She said every school assembly in Georgia started with "My Country 'Tis of Thee" but there were lots of patriotic songs, and she was going to teach us another one.

She picked a really good song, especially the chorus, which we sang as hard as we could. "Three chairs for the red, white and blue. Three chairs for the red, white, and blue. Oh the Army and Navy forever, three chairs for the red, white, and blue."

The song ended. We all sat down, still somewhat aquiver. Some of the first graders wiped their nose on the inside of their elbow as Mr. Donahue got up to read the Scripture verses. I knew I ought to listen, but the song kept dancing in my head. "Three chairs for the red, white, and blue. Three chairs...."

Suddenly, there I was on the Chatauqua stage. It was the closing night minstrel. I doffed my high, silver hat with a flourish.

"Ladees and Gentle-men, we bring for your en-ter-tain-ment tonight a little music, a little fun. Permit me to introduce myself. I am your interlocutor. And these gentlemen in the three chairs are Mr. Red, Mr. White, and Mr. Blue. Mr. Blue Bones, that is. Mr. Red, if you will kindly punch Mr. Blue Bones and wake him up, I'd like to ask him a question. Mr. Blue, will you please tell these folks, which came first, the chicken or the egg?"

Just then, Cora Ball punched me from behind with a sharp pencil point, changing my giggles at my own brilliance to a slight scream.

Mr. Donahue, ever tolerant of minor chapel misbehavior, ended the Scripture reading in his usual calm, preacherish tones.

"Suffer little children," he concluded, "for of such is the kingdom of heaven."

# The Shade of the Big Hickory Tree

The shade under the big hickory tree looked cool and dark. I sank down onto the ground and wished I had brought one of Mother's clean white linen handkerchiefs to wipe the perspiration away. It was a blistering day, and I wasn't halfway to the store yet. This was one of my favorite places along the way. Already, my hot legs were feeling better as I rubbed them over the soft, powder-white sand.

I could see two cows in Uncle George's pasture on one side of Bulloch Avenue. They were lying down chewing their cuds. On the other side of the road was Mrs. Penland's cotton patch. I had begged Mother to let me pick cotton until one day last fall she said to me, "All right, if it is a good day tomorrow, you may pick cotton, but I do not think you will last long."

I did last, though. I lasted until lunch time. But I will tell you this—cotton lint down the back of your dress is the worst itch in the world. When we stopped for dinner at noontime, I decided I'd picked enough. I asked for my money, and they weighed my bag. I made seventeen cents.

It wasn't cotton-picking time now though. It was the middle of summer and a lot hotter than November. Right where I was sitting there was a big cool patch of

white sand. I knew better than to do what I was about
to do. But I did it anyway. I took off one black patent
Mary Jane pump. Then I took off my white sock and
reached out and wiggled my toes in the white sand of
the sidewalk.

Oh, how good it felt! I did not do what I'd
intended and put my shoe back on. Instead, I took off
the other shoe and sock. I ran around and dug into the
sand. I lifted first one foot, then the other, and let the
warm sand trickle between my toes.

Suddenly, I remembered Mother had told me to hurry. "Honey, please run to the store and get me a dime's worth of sugar and half a dozen lemons. I want to get this gelatin dessert into the refrigerator so it will chill and set by supper time," she had said.

I decided not to waste time putting my shoes back on. Maybe nobody would notice, even though Mother often told people that on account of broken bottles and hookworm, she could not let her children go barefoot.

I started running, but had not counted on how the sharp rocks on Uncle George's hill would cut into my tender feet. When I got to the town square, the sidewalks were so hot I could not stand it. I stepped onto the grass, but it was full of stickers. I'll tell you, it was not any fun.

At last I got to the tin roofed porch in front of the store. Mr. Foster's surrey was tied up there. I would rather ride in the surrey than do anything. Coots and Belle were tossing their heads at the flies.

I walked into the store and started through the dry goods department. Miss Lizzie saw me and called out, "Hello, Virginia. Where's your mother? I have the prettiest piece of gingham for a dress for you. Bring your mother to see it, before it's all sold."

"Would you let me see it, Miss Lizzie?"

She reached toward the shelves and my heart sank. She was reaching for that piece of pink with the white lambs scattered all over it, some upside down. I did not know what to do. Mother was so tender-hearted she wouldn't want to hurt Miss Lizzie's feelings so she would buy it. Then I'd have to wear it and look like a baby. And I hated pink anyway.

"Miss Lizzie," I said real fast, "Mother told me to bring her some of that green plaid. See that piece with the little white and green and red checks."

Miss Lizzie frowned. "I don't think your mother would want that. It is too old for you. Laura Roberts got some of that piece last week for a dress."

Laura Roberts was sixteen and one of the prettiest girls in town.

"Yes, Mother told me, Miss Lizzie. She said to be sure to bring home a piece of that green plaid gingham."

Miss Lizzie cut off the fabric, and I breathed a sigh of relief. At least for now, I could forget the pink and white lambs. I watched the little basket run along the overhead wire to take the ticket back to Blanche Lowe, the cashier. After Blanche checked it, the little basket came racing back to Miss Lizzie's stop. She wrapped the ticket into the package.

I put the package under my arm and went back to the grocery section of the store. Mr. Rainwater always waited on Mother. I saw him behind the meat counter turning the new sausage mill. Big ropes of ground meat were coming out in a round circle.

"Are you making sausage in your new mill?" I asked conversationally.

"Hello, Virginia! he said. "No, I can't work pork when it is this hot, have to wait for hog killing time. This is good packinghouse beef. I expect your mother would like it. It came in today on the morning train."

If there was one thing in the world I loved, it was packinghouse beef, ground and broiled and nice and juicy.

"I know Mother will want some," I said.

"I'll be through here in a few minutes," Mr. Rainwater said.

While he finished, I picked up handfuls of coffee beans at the coffee barrel and let them run through my fingers. Then I got a measuring pot full of penny candy. "Please put this penny's worth of candy on Mother's charge," I said.

Mr. Rainwater was wrapping up the ground meat when Charlie Foster came in. The Fosters were our neighbors, and Charlie was nearly grown. He drove the horses and surrey all the time.

"Are you shopping for your mother this hot afternoon?" Charlie asked. "If you are ready to go home I'll give you a ride."

Not even riding in Mr. Foster's boat on the river could have been more fun than riding home this hot afternoon in the surrey. Charlie untied Coots and Belle, I hopped in, and we were off at a trot. I could feel the cool breeze running past my face. It seemed only a tiny jiffy later that the surrey was swinging around our driveway.

Mother came running out of the house. "Baby," she cried, " I was getting worried! I was about to set out looking for you. Thank you, Charlie, for bringing her home."

I was thinking about the green plaid material in

the package under my arm. "Probably she will stop calling me 'Baby' when I start wearing this," I thought.

It was only then I realized my mother was looking at me very sternly. "Virginia Wing," she said, "what have you got under your arm? It is certainly not a dime's worth of sugar, nor is it half a dozen lemons. And where are your shoes and socks?"

Mother talked to me for a long time. I cried and said I was sorry. And I was. But I soon smelled the packinghouse beef broiling for supper. Just as we were ready to eat, my father came in the front door, and I heard his voice cheerfully say, "Shoes and socks, all here and accounted for."

As I was going to sleep that night, I truly did try to figure out what had happened. But I could not think then, and I cannot think now, exactly how it came about.

# Webster's Blueback Speller

Just about my favorite place in the world to sit was in Daddy's lap. I felt so good and strong and safe there. Sometimes Tow and I both would sit in his lap, and he would tell us stories about animals. And sometimes he would sing songs like "Old Dan Tucker sang for his supper, combed his hair with a wagon wheel and died with a toothache in his heel."

"Looks like it's just you and me tonight," Daddy said. "Mother put Tow to bed with an outing flannel cloth soaked in hot Vicks salve on his chest. She thought his cough sounded a little croupy. And I'd say she is asleep over there on the couch. Spring housecleaning is hard even when you have good help.

"How would you like it if you and Daddy surprise them by learning some new words tonight?"

"I know where the Webster's Blueback Speller is Daddy. I saw Mother put it on a shelf in the whatnot. I'll go bring it."

I knew why my daddy had trouble spelling and writing and reading. When he was a little boy at Miss Pratt's school, they thought he didn't learn much because he was dumb.

And then, when he was nineteen years old, he went to Atlanta to an eye doctor. Old Doctor Calhoun was supposed to be the best in Atlanta. But he just said,

"I'm sorry, my boy, there is nothing I can do for your eyesight." Then as my daddy was walking down the street, he saw a sign made like a big pair of spectacles. He went in and was fitted with the glasses he is still wearing.

Mother told Daddy you are never too old to learn. She said he was lucky because he had the whole world of good books ahead of him. And she read to him a lot. I listened sometimes, but Tow never did because he was too little.

I got the Webster's Blueback Speller. And I had an idea.

"Daddy," I said, "I want to learn the longest word in the book."

Daddy burst out laughing. Then he hugged me. "You crazy little goose," he said. But he said it lovingly.

He looked through the book. "Here's one," he said. "In the section I've been working in. It may not be the longest, but it's long enough. Do you think you could learn to spell incomprehensibility?"

I won't say it was easy. But after a good deal of work, I got so I could rattle it off. It sounded something like this: I-n, in; c-o-m, com; incom; p-r-e, pre, incompre; h-e-n, hen; incomprehen; s-i, si; incomprehensi; b-i-l, bil, incomprehensibil; i-, i; incomprehensibili; t-y, ty, incomprehensibility.

When I had learned to spell it, my daddy said, "Now, do you know what it means? No? Well, it means something of which the meaning is not clear or which we cannot understand."

We learned a lot more words. And then one of the big pillows fell off the couch where Mother was sleeping.

"Bartow," she cried, jumping up. "Why did you let me sleep the whole evening away?"

"I am sure you needed it. Besides, Virginia and I have been studying my spelling lesson."

"I learned to spell incomprehensibility," I said. "I'll spell it for you."

"Just once," Daddy said firmly. "You need to be in bed, young lady."

Mother and I went into the bedroom. I got undressed and put on my beautiful new lacey nightgown that had no feet like those old Dr. Dentons.

I knelt down beside Mother's big brass bed to say my prayers. I asked God to bless our family and the cats and the dogs and the Indian runner ducks and the cows and old Maude, our horse. I finished the prayer I always said, and then I added something.

When I got into bed and Mother leaned over to say goodnight, she said, "Virginia, you asked in your prayer for integrity. Is that one of the words you and Daddy learned tonight?"

"Yes, and I can spell it, too."

"Do you know the meaning of integrity?"

"It means that you don't do something bad even if nobody is watching you. Daddy wants Tow and me to have it. But, Mother, I only asked for a little because I already have some. When you and Daddy are around, it's pretty easy to have it, but when I'm by myself, I think I need a little help."

Mother left me to go to sleep; and as she walked through the sitting room door, I heard her say to Daddy, "How do people without children face the commonplaceness of life?"

I was asleep almost before I could hear the sound of the door closing.

# Red Plush and Coal Smoke

### A Day in Atlanta

The creamy flare of the acetylene gaslights lit a circle on the porch, then faded into darkness against the tall columns. There was an unseasonable chill in the early September pre-dawn air. I pulled the sleeves of last spring's gabardine coat over my exposed wrists.

Aunt Annie called softly from the porch rocker where she was cooling off after the heat of the kitchen's wood stove.

"Virginia, did you button your shoes? All the way to the top?"

I hadn't, of course. The uppers felt so hard over my ankles after summer sandals.

"Then come right over here, young lady. I brought a button hook just in case."

Tow began to jump up and down. "Listen, Daddy! Daddy, listen! I hear the horses! Here it comes!"

"You're right, son. *Hattie, where are you?*"

My lovely Mother, looking flustered, came flying through the front doorway pinning on her sand-colored hat with the moss green velvet rouching just as the gray team thundered around the upper curve of the drive. The kerosene lanterns on each side of the hack flickered. Captain Hughes rasped his brake. We saw him stand up and yell, *"Whoa, Ben! Whoa, Pearl! Whoa, whoa. Whoa, now."*

The Irish showed clearly in my father. Love, laughter, and exasperation were in his voice.

"Hattie, if you are this late getting your cab to the Atlanta station this afternoon, you may find yourself and the children spending the night at the Kimball House. Trains don't wait."

Mother liked to have the last word. "The Roswell train did wait once, Bartow, as you very well know, when they held it for you ten minutes the morning you were leaving for our wedding."

"That," said my father gently, "was because Ike Roberts and Captain Sudduth knew if their train left without me that day, the wedding might be called off and the prettiest girl in Gainesville would never come to Roswell to live."

Mother smiled, and the Irish had won again.

"Don't worry, darling, have Maude and the buggy at the station to meet us at six."

Mother reached to give him a goodbye kiss, then called out, "Oh, Sister Annie, thank you so much for getting up to fix our breakfast. Bessie will be here at seven to clean up, and she will bring the little boys to get water from the well and fill the bedroom woodboxes. And the alum for the green tomato pickles is out. And Bartow, it was my hatpin. A thing that big, eight inches long! I couldn't find it."

The mounting step was down beside the hack. Daddy lifted me up and in with a fine swing, then hoisted Tow up top beside Captain Hughes. At six, Tow still thought he was helping drive the horses. I could faintly remember when I sat in the driver's lap and yelled "Gee" and "Haw." There were moments when I would have exchanged my eight years for just one more wonderful ride like that.

In the hack Mother was talking to the grownups, and I was listening, as we trotted down the mile-long hill and through the covered wooden bridge across the Chattahoochee River. Captain Hughes gave the horses a touch of the whip. We swept up on the other side of the river and stopped outside our little railway station.

It was so exciting! The train was pushed from Roswell to Chamblee and then pulled back on the homeward trip. We could see Captain Roberts, the engineer, in his cab. We could see the face of the fireman, already sooty, in the light of the open fire door as he stoked the coal, getting up steam.

Inside the depot waiting room, while Mother bought our tickets, Tow and I stood near the round, glowing little stove. It was dim in the waiting room and very hot. We watched with interest as the section hands and car loaders sizzled gobs of tobacco spit against the stove.

Almost immediately Mother was pulling us along. "Come, children, it's so terribly hot in here. Let's go out on the platform. The birds may be waking up."

"Yes," Tow said. "And that tobacco spit smells awful."

Even at six, I would have known better; and we wouldn't have gotten our arms yanked nearly out.

As soon as she got us outside, Mother told Tow, as she did so often, that he simply had to learn to think about other people's feelings. And about politeness.

Then Tow and I went to look at the piles of lumber that our daddy had in the station yard, ready for loading that day. It was because he had to supervise the lumber loading and be sure each piece was first class that he couldn't go with us to Atlanta.

Mother regretted exceedingly that it had worked out that way. She would not have taken us without Daddy but she had not been able to bear spending a whole day in the city shopping in August, and now we had to have school clothes, especially shoes and long winter underwear.

Tow was on top of one of the piles of lumber when the engine bell began to ring and the whistle blew. We heard Mother anxiously calling us. The voice of the conductor, Captain Sudduth, rang out with "All Abo'd for Dunwoody, Chamblee, connections for Atlanta and points South. All Abo'd."

We ran as hard as we could and were lifted up into the car. Mother followed us down the aisle holding her sand-colored serge suit skirt in one hand while brushing the pine resin and dirt from Tow's knees with the other.

It was chilly inside the car. The chandeliers were lighted, their oil flames dancing; and the windows were so dirty you could barely see through to tell that daylight was coming on. But how lovely it smelled! The car seats were red plush and tickled the back of your neck when you got on hot and hurried in summer. Now it was cool. There was a mysterious and thrilling shut-in odor. An odor of soot, coal smoke, mildew, and Mother's lilac toilet water.

Just as Mother said, "Hold on, children, we are about to start," the train gave a big jerk, and we were moving. Tow fell flat on his face. Mother picked him up and asked lovingly where her baby was hurt. But Tow almost never cried. He said it was only a bump on his funny bone, and didn't hurt the place on his forehead where he fell so hard last week he dulled the rock.

A button had been pulled off his Russian blouse. Mother told him he was going to look a sight walking down the street in Atlanta looking like that, but maybe she could get a needle and thread from Mrs. Jenkins in the children's department at J. M. High's.

Just then, Mother looked down at her feet. I had heard mother laugh and sing. I had heard her cry a few times. But never before had I heard my stylish, beautiful mother give a gasp like that. It was pure horror.

"Virginia," she said in a funny little strangled voice. "Look! I've still got on my Daniel Green felt bedroom slippers. Oh, what can I do? Suppose I should meet one of Daddy's Atlanta customers? Or anybody we know. What on earth can I do?"

A few tears slid down her nose. "Oh, darling, what will people think of me?"

The train was chuffing past the pines and oaks and sassafras trees. And my mother was sitting there looking sad. "It was so early," she whispered almost to herself. "And I wasn't really awake. And I lost my hatpin."

Nothing like this had ever happened to me before. It could ruin our beautiful day in Atlanta. I thought about that. And I began.

"Well, Mother, we won't get out at Dunwoody. And nobody you know ever gets on the train there. And at Chamblee, when we change to the Bell, you can take us way down the platform, like we wanted to play or something. And just before the Bell pulls out, when we hear the 'All Aboard,' we can run jump on. Then, when we get to Terminal Station in Atlanta, I'll keep walking right in front of you. If we meet someone, you can say, 'These are my children.'

"And they will look at Tow and say, 'Oh, that beautiful little boy. Those magnificent pansy-blue eyes he has!' And you can tell them how much prettier he was before his father, much to your regret, got his dutchboy bob cut short last spring. And after a while, they will look at me and say, 'Oh, and you have a little girl, too. How nice!' And by that time we will be in the big place where the horse cabs are. You can tell the driver, 'Please take us direct to Black's Shoe Store.' By the time we get there, it will be open. And you can buy some shoes and tell the man to wrap your bedroom slippers in the new shoe box.

"So please don't be sad, Mother dearest. We will soon be in Atlanta. Tow will buy lots of things with his dollar at Kress's, and we will go to the Alamo Number Two to see Pearl White and have lunch at Nunnally's Tea Room on Whitehall Street."

I watched my mother's face as I talked. Little by little she began to smile. When I stopped for breath, she took my hand and said, "Oh, Virginia, what would I do without you? Of course we'll have a lovely day. And I'm so proud of you. I never realized my little eight-year-old daughter could be so mature."

"Eight and a half," I said.

She smiled and answered, "Almost eight and a half. How fast you children grow up. I wish I could keep you just as you are now."

The train stopped for Dunwoody. Some people got on. But nobody we knew, just as I expected. Then the train started again, and I kept thinking, as we got up speed, and the wheels turned round, and the train leaned from side to side on the curves, "A-click, a-click, mature, mature" until the wheels seemed to be talking just to me. Mature meant grown up. Now I was mature. Mature people chose what they liked.

"Mother," I asked, "am I old enough for a middy blouse trimmed with red soutache braid and a blue serge pleated skirt?"

Mother patted my hand and thought we would see if they had them in my size. So I tried again.

"And for my shoes. Don't you think I'm mature enough for laced-up shoes, not buttoned ones?"

She laughed. "Laced-up shoes are for big girls. But, there, dear, don't worry. Maybe we can find some with low heels. And with laced shoes we'd never again have to hunt for the shoe buttoner. That would be nice."

I knew then, almost knew, that I'd get anything within reason that I wanted in Atlanta. But something deep inside told me not to mention the most important thing of all. I'd get it. I'd manage because it was vitally important. We would go home with twisted stick candy from Nunnally's and with the tiny lamb chops and thick porterhouse steaks Daddy loved from Mr. Pink Cherry's market. We'd have new coats and sweaters for school, and I was pretty sure my laced-up shoes would be under my arm in a shiny shoebox. But one thing we would not have. Not in all those packages would there be a single pair of hot, scratchy, detestable long wool drawers for me. If I froze walking to school next winter, I'd never say a word. I did not know how I'd manage it. But while Mother was buying a new one-piece corset at J. M. High's, I'd have time to think of a way.

I might be the only eight-and-a-half-year-old in Roswell School who didn't wear long drawers. But I'd do it. I'd think of a way, now that I was mature.

# Seat of Grace

My knees, below the hem of my white linen church dress, looked brown against the soft rosy plaid of our pew's cushion. Aunt Annie and Uncle Gene's pew was just behind ours. Sometimes I sat down in their pew before I realized it although I knew the difference because their cushion was covered in solid-color calico. Mother was not noted for being early, and if she came rushing in after we finished singing the Doxology, I'd just stay by Aunt Annie.

This school year I had received a New Testament with my name inside:

*Awarded to Virginia Wing*
*For One Year's Perfect Attendance*
*Roswell Presbyterian Sunday School*
*December 25, 1914*

My ninth birthday was coming soon, and I found I could read my Testament a little. I understood the "thees" and "thous" though not too many of the other uncommon words. But I could always find a verse I could read well enough to memorize and recite each Sunday.

Tow was too little to stay for church. He went outside and played with the other young children.

One or two mothers looked after them. When it rained they went inside the manse next door and told stories. But I had been staying for church for nearly two years now. Mother thought I was too young for it. Sometimes I did get tired as I craned to look up at Mr. Doak. By the time he climbed the steps to the high pulpit, I could just see head and shoulders. When he came down to the communion table and removed the snowy white, embroidered linen cloth that covered the big silver cup and tray of bread cubes, he looked human size again.

Today was Communion Sunday. While Mr. Doak was getting things ready, I tried to read the tablet behind him. It was white marble with a gold border and the letters, traced in gold, were *In loving memory of the Reverend Nathaniel A. Pratt, DD*. He had been the first pastor of the church long before I was born, back during the War Between the States. I couldn't read it all because Mr. Doak's body was in the way. I looked across the church and saw the ribbons on Mrs. Baker's little black mourning bonnet blowing in the spring breeze. Dr. Baker had been a pastor also, but I did not remember him either. Miss Lizzie Smith was the other lady who wore a black mourning bonnet with a veil, but her pew was at the back of the church, and I had my orders. It was in the poorest possible taste to turn around and stare at people.

Mr. Webb, our chief Elder, was passing the communion. I looked up, expecting to see the big silver cup. Instead, I saw a rack filled with the most wonderful little cups, tiny glass ones. Grape juice filled each cup. I felt Mother's hand on my knee and looked up to see her head shaking, a wordless sign she had for "No, you mustn't." I stopped my hand just in time and tried to look as if I meant to pick up the hymnbook laying next to me on the seat. But I was puzzled and a little hurt.

Surely those little cups were for children. After Mother swallowed the grape juice, she put her cup into a rack that had been fastened to the back of the pew in front of us.

I felt better by the time we had sung the final hymn. I loved to see Mrs. Garrison seated at the little organ, her head nodding in time with her busy arms and hands as she played. Her feet, just visible beneath her skirt, were pumping the pedals with a rhythm all their own. People were talking about getting a piano for the church. I hoped they wouldn't. Schools and homes had pianos, but the soft, squishy tones that came out of the organ were Sunday music.

We reached the church vestibule just as Maum Grace and Daddy William came down the steps from the old slave gallery. There were colored churches in town, but both of them had come to our church every Sunday of their lives, and nobody could persuade them to move from the gallery and sit downstairs. When Mother greeted them, Daddy William, who always wore a black suit and white shirt and stiff collar with a big gold chain across his vest, said to me "Lil' Missee big tis day."

"That's because I am nearly nine years old, Daddy William."

Maum Grace ducked her head in a bow and took my hand. She had on a starched purple dress and her Sunday white turban.

We stood on the porch and caught up on the news. The little children ran up and down the steps between the tall white columns as mothers began gathering their families. Daddy went around the church to where Maude had been left in the shade.

"Mother," I said as we walked through the grove, "why can't I take one of the communion cups? Why would they make them children's size and then not allow children to use them?"

"I don't know how to explain it, dear," Mother said. "When you are grown up and a church member, you will understand better. Now there is Sunday School and lots of things for you. But taking communion is only for members of the church. I am afraid I haven't really explained it very well." She sighed, and I saw her forehead wrinkle as it did when she was a little worried.

"But why do they have child-sized cups?" I asked.

"Oh, that is not the reason for the small cups. They are a new thing, sanitary communion."

Mother probably forgot it as we rode home along the dusty street. She had Tow in her lap and was chatting with Daddy. I was sitting in the back of the buggy with my legs drawn up under me to keep from catching the dust we kicked up. I kept thinking it didn't seem fair that old people like Mrs. Baker and Maum Grace and Daddy William could take communion. And I could get a New Testament and sing and put money in the little bean cup at Sunday School and be with the other grown-ups at church, but I couldn't take communion.

A few Sundays later, Mother had one of her sick headaches. When she had one, she went to bed in a darkened room with brown paper soaked in vinegar and black pepper on her forehead. Daddy telephoned Aunt Annie and arranged to have me walk with her and Uncle Gene to church. Tow stayed home.

After the sermon was over, Mr. Doak stood in front of the pulpit and extended an invitation to unite with the church. As he spoke, I felt he was looking straight at me. Nobody moved for a while. Then I did. I went up and shook hands and said that I would like to unite with the church.

When I went home, Mother was still in her darkened bedroom and did not feel like eating dinner. In the afternoon Daddy took Tow and me on a walk to teach us about trees. He showed us how to make slip whistles from pencil-sized poplar twigs. You can only do it in spring, but it makes the most beautiful high, loud noise.

By the time Mother got up, I had decided not to tell her about my plan to unite with the church but to surprise her instead.

Two weeks later, on the Sunday I was supposed to meet with the Session, Mother decided not to go to church. Daddy was away on a lumber-buying trip, and Mother thought it was too hot to walk in the broiling sun. I went to Aunt Annie's house, to walk with her. She said, "Your Uncle Gene tells me that you are to appear before the Session this morning, Virginia. Is that right?"

"Yes," I said. "But I am not sure why."

"They want to ask you some questions to be sure

your motives for joining the church are correct. Do you understand what that means?"

I answered that Mr. Doak had not mentioned motives when he said the door was open wide to all who wished to enter.

"And I wish to enter," I said. So Aunt Annie changed the subject.

All during Sunday School I felt nervous. I wondered why my heart seemed to jump. I almost forgot the verse I had memorized. The Sunday School hour seemed very slow, and Miss Evelyn told us a very long story. Finally, it was over but then I wished it were not.

When I walked out of the pastor's study where our children's class met, I saw six white-haired men sitting together by the big rosewood secretary. I knew there was a checkerboard inside one of the secretary doors that a wounded soldier carved during the Civil War when the church was a hospital. As I approached them Mr. Webb, the chief Elder, took my hand and led me to a chair.

"Virginia, you have indicated your desire to become a member of the Roswell Presbyterian Church. You are very young. The Session of the church must ask you some questions. If you do not understand these doctrinal questions, please tell us."

I understood the first questions. Then they asked me if I could repeat the shorter Catechism. I repeated the first two questions and answers and told them that was all we had to learn so far, but I could repeat the entire Children's Catechism. They thought that would

not be necessary. Then they got into hard questions like "Do you subscribe to the doctrine of predestination?"

I had no idea how to answer. "I know 'subscribe' is like you take the newspaper or a magazine. But 'predestination'? I got a Testament for Sunday School attendance. Can I look in there and tell you the answer?"

There was a buzz of conversation among the old men. They got books and records from the rosewood secretary shelves. They looked things up and discussed them in whispers.

Finally Mr. Webb said, "Virginia, it seems that our regulations allow the individual Session a good deal of freedom when considering those who may not completely understand theological doctrine as long as we are convinced that the candidate is sincere.

"However, you are very young. Wouldn't you rather wait a few years until you can better understand church doctrine?"

"If you tell me to, I guess I'll have to," I said. "But Miss Evelyn told us about how Jesus said to suffer little children to come unto me and forbid them not."

A smile went round. One of the old men spoke up. "I believe Virginia may be trusted to learn more about church doctrine as she gets older," he said. And they told me I would be received into the church at the morning service that day.

When the time came, I had to go down and stand in front of the pulpit. Mr. Doak sprinkled water on me, and it ran down my neck a little. The grown people passed by and extended the right hand of fellowship, and Aunt Annie hugged me and leaned over and kissed me. I was accepted as a member of the Roswell Presbyterian Church.

Now came telling Mother. As I walked in the front door I saw her sitting on the tall bookkeeper's stool Daddy had bought her, talking on the telephone. She rang off in a hurry and rushed to me. "Darling, why didn't you tell Mother you were going to join the church today? Why didn't you tell me?"

"I don't know, Mother. I did mean to tell you. But it was something I did, not you."

She looked thoughtful. "I do think Sister Annie might have told me," she said.

But I did not think so. And now I look back and think Aunt Annie was right to recognize my privacy.

An unexpected thing happened on the next Communion Sunday. When Mr. Webb passed the rack of little glasses to our pew, I took one. I drank the Welch's grape juice it contained. But I hardly tasted the liquid that was sparkling in the light. I had a feeling I had never had before, like happiness flooding through my body.

I thought to myself, "I'm not too young." As I put the empty little glass into the rack in front of me, I barely remembered how much I had wanted to just hold it a few weeks earlier. For something was happening to me that had nothing to do with a child's toy.

# Mimosa Seat

It was a beautiful November day, a day when summer had momentarily come back. I was disappointed when Mother refused to go with Daddy to the barbecue at Acworth to celebrate the opening of the new topsoiled highway.

"Bartow, I just don't think I can go," she said. "I am making my annual three-day green tomato pickle, and this is the second day. You have to go because you are chairman of the county commissioners. You take Tow with you and Virginia can go on to school."

As an eleven-year-old eighth grader, I was finding Latin and algebra hard. I did not have much room for argument. So I stayed and went to school as usual.

Our class was just marching out for recess when my cousin, Edith Rucker, found me. "Virginia, honey, you must come with me quick. Your daddy has been in an accident."

We went outside. Nap, Edith's husband, was there in his Buick. Nap was a baseball pitcher for Brooklyn and won the World Series one year. Usually I would have been thrilled to ride in the Buick.

But now I seemed to be somewhere else, looking on. Daddy and Tow were in the hospital in Marietta.

A train had hit their car, and Glenn Coker, who was driving them, had been killed.

The standing off and watching myself got worse. I spent the night on a cot in the hospital. Next morning they told me we were going home, my father had died.

Somebody in my shape rode home to Roswell. Somebody watched the yard fill with buggies and wagons and autos.

Somebody said politely, "No, thank you, I don't want to see him once more."

Somebody, after everyone had left, sat on the corner base of one of the porch columns, with words from a story she had read going through her mind for the thousandth time: "Too deep for tears." Too deep for tears. Too deep. Too deep. They all thought I was heartless, but I couldn't cry. Too deep for tears.

I still had on my best dress and the new ribbed white silk stockings that made me feel so grown up. I walked to the end of the porch, to my mimosa tree with the high limbs that forked into a seat.

My mimosa seat, the special place I loved. All summer I had hidden there among the leaves and sweet blossoms. I would tie a string around my book, shimmy up the tree, and pull my book up after me, spending blissful hours reading in a private world.

Now I had to be there. The lacy dress made climbing hard. But at last I was safely in my seat, feeling the familiar curve of the tree limbs. I looked up and around and down. Just beneath me was the hitching post, its chain dangling loosely.

Then I saw my father drive up in the buggy,
Maude's coat shining from the currycomb and brush. I
heard him call, "Hattie, you and the children come on.
Let's drive down to the river. Lilies ought to be
blooming on the bluff." I saw him leap from the buggy,
hitch Maude, and bound toward the house.

At last I wept profusely, almost losing hold of the tree, my tear-wet cheeks scratched by the rough bark. When the tears finally stopped, I was no longer looking at someone else in my body. I was myself in my mimosa chair. There was a snagged hole in my new silk stockings.

I thought, "Mother won't have much money without Daddy. I'd better fix this."

I climbed down carefully and went into the house. I found a needle and some white cotton thread and painstakingly drew the torn place in the stocking into a small, tight lump. It didn't look like much since I knew nothing about darning. But I knew that now I must meet problems as best I could.

# The Touch of A Butterfly's Wing

Two gorgeous azure and black butterflies were perched at the end of our back porch shelf where I was washing my hair. Their wings were spread in a symphony of velvet. I had carefully set my china bowl and pitcher at the other end of the shelf so as not to disturb them.

It seemed to me I was feeling everything more in this summer when I was sixteen. I thought how fragile the butterflies were and how a single blow could end their joyous, short lives.

I poured water from the china pitcher and mixed in the boiling water I'd heated on the kitchen wood stove. I was washing my hair a few days early. I knew the Power family was moving into our spare-room apartment today, and I wanted to look devastating for their son, George.

I knew very little about him except that he was eighteen and leaving soon for his junior year at the University of Pennsylvania Wharton School. I was starting out as a freshman at Agnes Scott College. There was little chance he would remember me when surrounded by a bunch of knowledgeable Yankee girls.

I sighed through the soapsuds.

But the morning was lovely and the butterflies were still there. I poured on another dabble of shampoo and scrubbed hard, using lots of water. I wanted my hair to shine.

Water ran down my dress and big gobs of soapsuds stuck to my face. I was wearing my Cinderella dress, faded, shapeless, and torn. I saved it for messy jobs like this one. I shut my eyes and scrubbed.

I have had a few surprises in my life. But never such a shock as now greeted me. Two hands on my shoulders whirled me around and then, as soft as the wing of a butterfly, a kiss swept lightly down my cheek.

Before I could think, I felt my tennis-playing right arm swing into a slap that was not light. I found myself facing him. "You mind your own business, George Power."

He brought the back of his hand to his cheek, which was beginning to turn red. There was a look in his eyes I could not interpret. I began to feel ashamed. Never in my life had I hit anyone hard.

"I'm sorry," I said. "Does it hurt much?"

"I'll recover," he said, and turned and walked into the house.

I finished washing my hair, put away the utensils, and went to my room where I rolled my damp hair on kid curlers.

I spent most of the day working on my clothes. But I was in a state of internal turmoil.

Why had he done it? Did he plan to do it? But most of all, how could he have wanted to kiss anybody that looked as awful as I did in that torn and faded dress with soap all over my head?

By afternoon I felt better so I got dressed and carefully combed my freshly curled hair. I went into the front hall bedroom and looked out the window. George was on the porch. Alone. I decided to go down.

I walked out the front door and we looked at each other wordlessly.

Then Professor Power came out.

"Papa," George said with great assurance, "I have just asked Virginia to go for a spin in the flivver with me. Is that all right?"

"That's fine, Son," Mr. Power said, "provided you are home on time. This will be our first night's supper at Bulloch Hall, and your mother wants us all present and accounted for."

We were down the front steps in an instant. George lifted me over the running board onto the seat of the flivver, and we were off.

"Why did you tell your father you had asked me to go riding when you had not mentioned it to me?" I said. "You knew I couldn't refuse without being ungracious."

"I had planned to," he said. "But I was afraid if I asked, you'd turn me down. Miss Wing, would you go for a ride around beautiful Roswell with me?"

I'd be delighted," I answered.

# The Chairs Not Sat In

As my roommate and I entered the college chapel, we could see two empty chairs on the stage. Excitement flooded through me. I was a full-fledged college student, and I was trying out for membership in Blackfriars, the college Dramatic Club.

From the years when I had kept a diary labeled *My Book of Interesting A Vents* and had written in it of "entertainments" given for family and friends, I had wanted to be an actress.

Tonight was my opportunity. The senior who admitted us to the auditorium whispered, "One more before you. Sit anywhere, your names will be called."

Bebe and I sat down and watched two of our classmates step up to the platform, play scripts in hand. They sat in the chairs and began to read a scene from "The Wild Duck" by Henrik Ibsen.

I whispered to my roommate, "They will probably get in. Miss Gootch loves Ibsen's plays."

Bebe gave me her gentle, blue-eyed smile, thought the matter over carefully and said, "Miss Gootch won't like it if you whisper."

Bebe hadn't wanted to be my partner in the tryout. "I'll probably be so scared I'll fall down going to the stage," she said.

"You won't be scared," I said.

"How do you know?"

"Because I am going to train you so well you will feel nothing but assurance."

We practiced a lot. Every night we went into the hall bathroom where the lights were not turned off automatically at ten o'clock as they were in our room. This was not exactly legal so we had to be very quiet.

In spite of all I did to keep her energy level up, Bebe occasionally dropped off to sleep. How she could do it, I could not understand. For I had found the most marvelous excerpt from a scene by Edna St. Vincent Millay. The two characters were Columbine and Pierot, and the scene was tender and yet sophisticated.

"I believe you feel about Edna St. Vincent Millay like Miss Gootch does about Ibsen," Bebe said. "But you know this wasn't on the approved list of tryout possibilities."

Sometimes Bebe provoked me. "That is our purpose," I said. "We have chosen a very modern piece which we will do without scripts."

"But," she said, "we are supposed to read it."

"We will have it memorized," I said, "and that will free us to act out our parts."

All that was in the past. Now we were at the crucial moment, and I was feeling a little nervous. I tried to think about my great success in Roswell school plays as Lady Macbeth and Queen Isabella. How regal I had looked!

Miss Haslam and Miss Wing were called to the stage. The president of the Dramatic Club was sitting near the steps.

"Have you got your scripts?" she whispered helpfully.

I gave her a deprecating smile. "We know our parts," I said.

"*Move the chairs*," I stage whispered to Bebe.

Bebe moved the chairs, as she had been directed to do in many a late-night rehearsal, and assumed a crouching position with her back to the audience.

Columbine was smelling the flowers. Now Pierot entered playing on the pipes of Pan. Pierot alternated music and poetry honoring his true love. I kept the music as short as possible because all we had been able to find as a musical instrument was a police whistle and it made a rather penetrating sound.

Finally Pierot spied his lovely Columbine and with a glorious sweep, drew her to her feet. The two of them waltzed once around the stage. Then he pushed her away from him at arm's length. Although his Columbine was half a head taller, he looked up and delivered to her an impassioned love poem. At the end of it Columbine was to speak her first lines.

But instead, there was silence. Pierot tried to ad lib. The silence continued. Then, "What do I say?"

I began for her. "Ah, Pierot," came out in a husky whisper. "Now what?" Then more silence, and more. Until at last Columbine gave up. With her hands over her face she ran down the steps, through the audience, and into the night. I tried to maintain a little dignity. I pushed the empty chairs back into place. Then walking as gracefully as I could, I headed for the door. Miss Gootch was waiting.

"Miss Wing," she said, "didn't you know this was to be a reading of a scene from one of the plays I suggested? And that stage action was not called for?"

I broke in. "Yes, Miss Gootch, you told me those things, but you see, I thought..."

Miss Gootch sighed. "That," she said, "is always the trouble."

I did graduate from that college. And I kept the same roommate though I cannot understand how she endured me.

But it has taken fifty years to really appreciate Miss Gootch's closing lines.

# The Green Morris Chair

The best looking, most sophisticated man I knew was coming to town to spend the weekend with his sister. Actually, he was coming to see me, and I was in such a state of excitement I kept him waiting thirty minutes for our date while I dithered whether I looked better in the blue georgette or the flesh pink crepe de chine.

When I went into the living room, I found him sitting in the green Morris chair before the fire Mother had made. There were jonquils on the mantel, and it was April. But it was a horrible night. He was telling Mother it had taken almost seven hours to drive from Chattanooga.

"Usually," he said, "the flivver will make it in a little over five hours, but we had two flats, and then we had to drive into Atlanta."

"We?" I said brightly. "Who is we?"

"Oh," he said in an extremely offhand way, "just a girl I know. Just a friend."

By now Mother had stayed long enough to be polite, so she excused herself, saying that Tow was in the kitchen making fudge. He'd bring us some to sample in a little while, she added.

When she left the room, we looked at each

other rather hungrily. But we were not thinking of fudge. I was still miffed and uncertain about "just a girl I know." I became very impersonal.

"Would you like to see some Kodak pictures I made recently?" I asked.

"Well, I guess so. Who are they of?"

"Oh, not you," I said sweetly. "But of a very charming gentleman."

I got the pictures and with a flirt of crepe de chine skirt just happened to perch on the arm of the Morris chair. I leaned down and handed him a picture of our old hound dog Trail, sitting, as was his choice, in one of the front porch rockers.

"You little devil," he said. My heart did a flip and suddenly there were two of us in the Morris chair.

Human conduct is sometimes a strange riddle, especially one's own. That chair subconsciously represented convention and family restraint to me. My father had sat there with his hands grasping the lion-head chair arms. When the minister came to call, he sat there. The family doctor sat there while he took my temperature and looked at my tongue.

I'd found the only man I wanted. But though clear thinking was impossible, I knew I had to say "no." It was a long and stormy session with much talk of "self respect" and "respect for each other," and "what is the real meaning of love?"

When my brother came in with the fudge, the look he saw on our faces made him hurriedly set the plate down and leave. By the end of the evening we were emotionally exhausted, but we had the most precious of gifts. We had begun to know each other as human beings.

It was two Aprils later on a lovely afternoon that he arrived to take me to the opera in Atlanta. He was driving a magnificent new Essex coup. He felt good about his job because he had just gotten a twenty-five dollar monthly raise. He said he could not spend all that money alone, and he placed upon my willing finger a gorgeous square diamond.

That was 1928. A good many years have passed. The Morris chair moved to my brother's home in California, passing down on the male side of the family as it should have. On our visits there, my husband would look at the chair with a twinkle in his eye and say, "Do you know, dear, I sometimes wonder if we didn't miss a good deal on account of your silly ideas about that chair."

I would smile but never answer. And the two wooden lion-head arms continue to wear their same sphinx-like grin.

## A Love Poem

You could write a love poem just like that?
Crash! I love you.
Well, you might color it up a little
With some overtones of sex.
An occasional break of boredom,
My Mama told me to be a good wife.

But where are moments like the morning
After you returned from two years
Overseas, and said to me,
"Get up, and bring me my socks from the dresser."
And I said, "Let your bearer do it."

How do you fit into days when your laughter
Got me through the dismal slogging?
Nights when I tossed with whirling black
Swirls of caring and you needed sleep
To make a sale next day?

How did you know, as we got into the car
For church last Sunday,
To give me a careful, critical once over, then come out
    with
"That's a good suit on you."
Did you sense my shoulders needed straightening?
It worked.

Just as your eyes told, that time I almost died,
That you'd be around the corner.
"Come for a walk," you say, "to the top of the hill
    and back."
You and I and our dog climb the hill together.
Chuckling, crispy autumn leaves
Blow into our faces. A family.

Crash! A love poem?
Didn't you know? It takes sixty years.

# A Pretty Good Woman

George and I were coming into Chattanooga, returning from our glamorous North Carolina mountain honeymoon. Soft evening was descending, and it seemed that a curtain of light blanketed the city across the river and below us.

From this, my first opportunity to know the small city where I would spend the rest of my life, I learned some important things about my man and about myself.

Even on his honeymoon, my husband was a worker. He made for me, I learned, a trip delightful with all the joys of the mountains and luxury resort hotel living. But now, that was ending. I knew that I was coming back to earth.

The night was blistering inside the city. No air conditioning tempered the heat in those days, and I was faced with one of the most dismaying sights a young woman can face. I was going to live temporarily in an apartment that belonged to my mother-in-law. A dusty young woman with a line of brown across my cheeks, I surveyed my new world and found it wanting.

Fast food restaurants in our part of the world were limited to sandwich bars in drug stores. It was up to my waiflike self to cook our dinner. I immediately sent my husband to the Vine Street Market.

He returned with two filet mignons two inches thick, one medium-sized yellow squash, and a few handfuls of green beans, plus a small can of sliced carrots. Since I had never heard of cooking vegetables less than half an hour, I decided we would eat the canned carrots and steak. We finally had dinner in that small apartment. It is hard to ruin a filet.

I picked up a little cleaning experience as the months went by. And I developed a ring-worm sore on my knee when I tried to modernize the kitchen floor with a dishrag. In this way I met Charlie Homan, a doctor who was my strong right arm for several years.

Charlie was a friend, and he had a magic medicine—Dr. Homan's pink panacea for puny people. He saw me through kidney stones, and George found Charlie's advice especially to his taste.

"Ginny," Charlie said to me, "your rule about how much to drink should be as follows: any time anybody hands you a drink, you hand it to George." Naturally, George found this advice easy to take.

Prohibition-induced drinking led to an afternoon on the mountain one hot summer day. My husband asked, "How would you like to go to Signal Mountain and pick up a keg of the very best corn liquor?"

"Good," I said. "And I hope it will be cool up there."

We wound our way up the W Road to the top of the mountain and drove through gorgeous summer-blooming rhododendron before finally stopping at a little store. A man was seated in a rocking chair out front, looking pleased with the world and with himself.

"Howdy, Oscar," my new husband said.

Oscar continued rocking peacefully.

"How 'bout the keg I left you?"

"All ready. Good corn," Oscar sniffed.

"Good." my husband said. "Well, Oscar, I told you I was going to get married. This is my wife."

I have never received a more intensive, head-to-foot going over. Oscar turned, directed a well placed "spat" of chewing tobacco away from traffic, and said in a slow, reserved tone, "Well it looks like you got yourself a pretty good woman."

This was followed by a spat of chewing tobacco in the opposite direction.

# The Chair That Burned

The next chair I remember was the one that burned. We were coming out of the aftermath of the great depression of 1929 and were beginning to relax a little. We called each other Walsie from some now forgotten, but excruciatingly funny occurrence that had to do with the term Palsie Walsie.

We were living in a snug little furnished house for which we paid $30 per month rent. We did all upkeep. I had even joined the Girls' Cotillion Club. For the night of the Christmas fancy-dress party, I had rather recklessly invited six couples to come by our house before the dance.

I looked around our living room, and although I was thankful we had a roof over our heads, I realized it looked pretty shabby. Our beautiful gray-green sofa, the only piece of furniture we had bought, sat beside the fireplace. Right across was a sad looking chair, its white muslin undercover showing through the frayed black satin upholstery. When I went to Watson's Salvage Store to hunt material for my dance costume, I decided I'd keep my eyes open for something with which to slipcover that chair.

I hit the jackpot on both counts. When I found some lovely, deep green velvet, I instantly pictured myself as Robin Hood's Maid Marian. I could make a green doublet and a peaked hat trimmed with the gorgeous wine-purple ostrich plume Mother had given me from an old hat of hers. I bought what I needed for the costume, including a pair of cotton long drawers that I planned to dye forest green for my medieval hose.

Then I found the perfect material for the slipcover. It was a linen-like texture with a soft brown background and a big splashy design of field flowers in burnt orange, white, yellow, and a little blue. How it would light up that living room with its musty old taupe rug!

"You will need enough to match the design," the helpful saleslady told me.

"To do what?" I asked. My experience in making slip covers was very limited.

"Oh, you know, you have to center a bouquet in the middle of the back and on the seat cushion."

I thought quickly and decided I could buy one and three-quarters yards more than I'd measured for and still have car fare left to get home.

While she was cutting the material, the saleslady said casually, "You will need two spools of brown thread."

There went my car fare dime. I walked to Walsie's office and waited to ride home with him, all the time planning how I'd make the new things. It was only a week until the party. I'd have to get going.

The morning of the party dawned, if you could call it dawn. It was snowing briskly. Visibility was zero when Walsie left for the office at 7:15. I breathed a prayer that he wouldn't get stuck on the Barton Avenue hill, even as I set a new batch of green dye heating. My medieval hose had come out lettuce colored the first time. The rest of the costume was ready.

The hors d'oeuvre mixes were in the refrigerator, except for the marinated fresh vegetables. That would take time. And the slipcover was far from finished. Fitting and matching patterns was more difficult than I had anticipated. I sewed and ripped and tried again, determined it should look professional.

At 5:45 Walsie finally got home, having slid all over North Chattanooga trying to make it. He bathed and dressed and put out Cokes and ginger ale and the special velvet-smooth corn we had been agitating in its charred keg in the attic for six months. Walsie didn't want a costume and I was glad, he looked so devastatingly handsome in his tuxedo.

At 6:05 I put the last stitch in the chair ruffle, closed the door of the back bedroom on the mess, and jumped in the shower. With unbecoming haste I began converting a modern miss of the thirties into a "right lovesome maid" of Arden Forest.

There was one problem. The medieval hose were now a lovely, deep green, but they sagged. The legs hung in wrinkles at the ankles and the seat hung down below the velvet tunic in a most unglamorous fashion. What to do? I grabbed a needle and thread, pulled everything up to my bra line, and sewed it firmly in place. The doorbell rang to signal the first guests.

It was almost a perfect evening. Everyone raved about the quality of Walsie's corn. You could drink it in a civilized way in tall glasses with ginger ale instead of having to chase it down with salt and lemon and a big glass of water before you could breathe again.

The only trouble was Martha. She was costumed as a milkmaid in yards of black and white striped skirt and a mop cap. All evening she sat in the new chair, skirts spread, hiding the chair completely. People brought her fresh drinks and lights for her cigarettes. And Martha sat. I was too shy in those days to think how I could get Martha out of that chair.

Finally someone said we'd better leave for the club or we wouldn't get a table. The others left, and I went to powder my nose while Walsie banked the furnace and put out our white tom cat, Diana. We met again in the living room. He sensed a crisis. "What's the matter?"

"Oh, my," I wailed. "I'm sewed in. Completely and irrevocably sewed into this thing." We both laughed until our sides ached. "Go get the scissors and some safety pins," he said, when he could talk.

With me pinned in, a more tenable situation for a long evening, we were ready to leave. But suddenly we smelled something burning. I looked at the newly covered chair and saw a widening cigarette-shaped hole. Smudgy smoke was coming out of the loose seat cushion's filling.

"Stop sniffling," said my masterly husband as I began to cry. "That's why we have this snow on the ground."

He carried the smoking cushion to the front door and threw it into the snow. We went to the dance and had an unforgettably delightful and carefree evening. Next day, I rescued the cushion, appliqued a matching patch over the hole, and felt sure nobody would ever notice it.

As has been said, there is simply no substitute for youth.

# Two Chevrolet Bucket Seats

When World War II started, we had been married thirteen years. A lifetime we called it. As octopus tentacles of war tightened around us more each day, Walsie struggled in never-never land as an officer at the Pentagon.

I struggled to preserve a semblance of our accustomed life. After moving five times, we finally had a Washington apartment, but it was unfurnished, and you could not buy decent furniture. Metal had gone to war.

Walsie came in looking bushed. It was spitting rain and snow outside.

"Do you remember we are supposed to have dinner with Shirley and Brian and then pick up the automobile chairs? The carpenter shop should have finished putting the legs on the chairs today."

"Not tonight," he said. "Oh, not tonight."

"But we've got to. The man is doing us an immense favor to put legs on those old Chevrolet bucket seats. So are the Houstons in getting him to do it. I hope we have enough gas to get there and back."

"We have gas," he said. "We won't be needing much more."

"Why not?"

"Because I'm ordered overseas. It's a two-year assignment. You know I couldn't turn it down."

We rode home after dinner with the two chairs in the back of the Chrysler, not saying much. I could hear the sleet hitting the windshield.

How strange it was. Only a few days ago I'd been so pleased with my idea of looking in an automobile boneyard for seats with real springs. Shirley had helped find a workman to convert them to chairs. I even had material to cover them. But now I knew, knew with what seemed more than a premonition, that we would never use those chairs. He would not come back to sit on them.

After four sleepless nights I took the wafers the Pentagon doctor had sent, and I slept like one drugged, which, of course, I was. The next morning I knew what I would do. I was going to get into whatever service would have me and go overseas, too. Neither my husband nor my mother liked the idea, but each recognized my right to decide.

On the day before Christmas, I saw him off, watching his plane fade into the ice-blue winter sky. Then I went back to the apartment and with a desperate need for activity, began to fit the covers onto the automobile chairs. I finished them while I was taking my Red Cross overseas training at American University. The Army shipped them to my mother's house in Georgia with the rest of our furniture.

I was one of a group of women herded with great secrecy across a midnight-darkened pier onto the Queen Mary. Once the great anonymity of the

European theatre of war swallowed me up, there remained one constant thin joy. From far off India a letter was sent each day, although they arrived in batches, once forty in a bunch. They told me (circuitously, to get around censorship) that he was living in a palace and was feeding peacock sandwiches to VIP's who visited from stateside.

The fortunes of war were different for me. First, I dished out doughnuts and coffee to American troops around England. Then I learned to drive a big truck. When D-Day occurred I was in buzz-bombed London teaching other girls truck driving.

I was then assigned to a hospital ship as a recreation worker and bounced around the English Channel on a converted ferry boat, bringing American wounded back from the French beaches.

Finally, I was given a permanent assignment with a field hospital, a small unit always near the front lines. During the Battle of the Bulge, our hospital was the only one in the area, and we narrowly avoided being captured.

## Midnight on the Rhine

Strange, I do not hear the guns
Across the Rhine,
But only the nightingale.
Shivering at a window
Every nerve cries fear
While others sleep.
Home, a dream,
Sea lengths away.
I know now that I wept
Not for war,
Or terror,
But for the nightingale.

## Square Notes Against the Fog

Square fields.
The last of the light is going.
Square notes.
The cuckoo cries into dimness.

Cuckoo.
Neat bird, definite bird.
Sneaky though.
Nest stealer.

Tell me what you say.
Will you listen for more?
Our world is at explosion's edge.
In England, in the long hedgerows,
We wait for cuckoo's notes,
Square notes against the fog.

# A Hospital Christmas During the Battle of the Bulge

Sgt. Rhodes and Sandy and I had been to the shell that was all that remained of the enlisted men's barracks. We went to see Beauty and her pups. Beauty was everyone's pet, an English fox hound who had come across the Channel with our hospital into eastern France and now into Belgium.

When the near-miss bomb hit the field by the barracks the night before, two miracles occurred. All the men were on duty because patients were pouring in like crazy, and there was no time for anybody to sleep. So no one was hurt even though the explosion took out every floor of the building, leaving only the framework and several flights of stairs intact.

Beauty and her pups were beneficiaries of the second miracle. Under the stairs in a box, they were a proud mother and happy babies, covered with a layer of plaster dust that bothered them not at all.

Today was Christmas Eve, and it was brilliantly sunny. As we crossed the street to the hospital, we saw people looking at a dogfight in the blue sky above. Parachutes opened beneath the bursts of smoke and flame. Sgt. Rhodes ran to his motor pool to get ambulances across the fields in a search for survivors.

Sandy and I hurried on to the hospital. Sandy was an enlisted man assigned as my assistant. He was a tough redhead from Brooklyn who knew how to laugh and how to fight. With the patients he was gentle as a lamb.

I was the lone Red Cross recreation worker assigned to the 46th Field Hospital attached to First Army in Northern Europe. As an advanced railhead was captured and secured, we moved on and served as a collecting station, sending back trainloads of patients to base hospitals in the rear.

We had been able to evacuate patients this morning, luckily, because 800 were crowded into the warehouse that was our hospital building. Now we were left with about 250, and that was still more than our TO called for.

As far as we knew, the Battle of the Bulge was still going. Streams of fleeing civilians hampered the military retreat. It had been like this for days, an eerie nightmare obscured by the dirty freezing fog that covered our world. Today's fair skies turned the tide; the clear weather permitted our planes to go into action. We knew the northern shoulder of the bulge was eight miles south of us with miles of enemy-held territory stretching out, below, and behind us.

As Sandy and I moved through the hospital wards, a patient asked me to write a letter for him. "Tomorrow will be Christmas day," he began. "How I wish I could be there to hear Tommy's voice when he sees his Santa Claus."

He did not tell his family that a shell burst had made him totally deaf. And, of course, I would never know if he recovered his hearing. In those days almost all stories were unfinished.

Back at my desk I found a surprise. "You wanted Christmas stockings," said the note I found from the hospital dentist. "Here they are. Don't ask questions. These were liberated. Now it's up to you to fill them." There was a stack of gleaming plastic bags beside the note.

So we launched "Operation Santa Claus," knowing we had one day in which to complete it. I sent out a plea for volunteer helpers while Sandy went to our Red Cross supply closet to bring chewing gum, cigarettes, razor blades, washcloths, stationery, and anything that might help to fill the bags. I went to see the mess sergeant. We considered Sgt. Wilson the best mess sergeant in the entire European theatre. But he looked glum when he heard my story.

"Mrs. Power, we have some oranges and apples and some hard candy. We had planned to put them at the hospital staff enlisted mens' places at lunch tomorrow. We have enough turkeys for the officers' lunch. And that is it. Only one supply truck came through."

Then he looked at me with his nice little twisted, friendly grin. "But if the CO should happen to give his permission...." I did not wait to hear the last words.

"Look, Ginny," the CO began, "You know as well as I do that we've had no mail in weeks, no gifts or food from home. Everyone is almost exhausted. We thought these holiday touches on Christmas day would give our people a little lift. But..."

I began to smile inside.

"I'll tell you what. The Pentagon would probably flip if they knew our democratic processes. But they are in Washington, the lucky so and so's. You and Sandy take a canvass of our personnel at lunch today. If the consensus is to do it, you've got my permission."

"Yes, Sir," I said. And ran into the door in my haste to leave.

Sandy and I waited until after lunch to ask. As each man approached the cans of suds to wash his mess kit, we put forth the question. The answer was yes, and yes, and yes, all down the line. I headed for the kitchen to break the news.

"Have a cup of coffee while you calm down, Mrs. Power," one of the young cooks said to me. While I drank the coffee, I began to think about the turkeys. Sgt. Wilson said it would have to be another case of five loaves and three fishes.

"But believe me," he said, "our turkey casserole will stretch to feed 250 patients. And oh yes, there is plenty of cranberry. The usual snafu. Not enough turkey but cranberry running out our ears."

Back at my desk, pandemonium reigned. The boys from the mess arrived with fruit and hard candies. All of headquarters joined to stuff Christmas bags. The chief administrative officer arrived with a large roll of bright red cotton tape.

"Tie 'em up with this," he said. "For the first

time in history, Army red tape is going to accomplish something."

Sometime past the hour of midnight, Sandy and I finished arranging and organizing the bags for distribution next morning. We had fashioned a large box to be slung across my shoulders with a piece of the red tape. One of the nurses donated her only Christmas token to decorate the box, a colored cutout of Santa Claus.

I was afraid at this late hour to head for the home of the Belgian family where I was quartered. Rumor had it German paratroopers had been dropped into our area. And there was a curfew on. So I found a vacant cot in one of the wards and stretched out fully clothed.

Next morning I was awakened by a voice from the next cot. A soldier was calling, "Nurse, nurse, come here quick. I must be having hallucinations. I think I see an American girl in the cot beside me."

"Don't you believe it, Soldier," I smiled. "You are looking at Santa Claus. Merry Christmas!"

And it was a Merry Christmas. As Sandy and I passed through the wards distributing those little bags, faces were filled with looks of disbelieving delight. We hinted there would be turkey for lunch. Some of the men began to sing carols. Everywhere there was conversation and laughter. Many of the men were already writing the folks back home on the stationery we had folded into air mail stamped envelopes.

As for us, we could hardly have presented a less Christmas-looking picture. The volunteers had tired eyes and wrinkled, slept-in uniforms. The officers and enlisted were eating beans. But very good beans, for Sgt. Wilson had a way with food. And there was plenty of cranberry. Here, too, faces had a delighted look. I don't suppose any of us will forget that day.

Just after lunch, one of the young cooks approached. "Want to go with me?" he asked. He was holding a small dish that contained just a taste of the turkey casserole. I followed him across the sunlit street into the empty shell that had been the barracks building.

He set the dish down for Beauty, still sheltering her pups beneath the disconnected stairs that now led to nowhere. As I looked up I could see the everlasting light of Christmas hope shining through those empty stairs.

A month after the war was over in Europe I was back in Washington, sneaking onto a crowded train without a ticket. I was headed for Georgia where my brother was home from the South Pacific. I found a seat in the lounge car. I still remember the brakeman's admonition during the night.

"Wake up Miss, and take your feet off the furniture. I'm sorry, but we have to have a rule. Sometimes people put their big, greasy feet on these nice chairs."

"Chairs," I thought. "The automobile chairs will be at Mother's."

The day before Christmas I met him in Washington. Two years to the day. The longest, and yet the shortest two years we had ever known. He resigned from the Army a full colonel, recently of the India Burma General Staff.

He came home to start over in a tiny business. I proudly showed him the nest I had made while awaiting him—a converted garage apartment with white ruffled curtains. I'd even wangled a telephone. We sat in the old Chevrolet bucket seat chairs and talked of gratitude, and home. Those automobile seats have been our favorite chairs now for a second half of a busy life time.

# Victory

There is no more exciting thing than greeting a future you firmly believed would never happen. But my husband and I began to establish a business and life together again. Just before his return, I'd bought two acres of hillside in the new, discreetly expanding area George irreverently called "Far East Riverview." It was beautiful land, but totally untended.

We erected a prefab in one corner of our new property and lived in a space so tight the living room chairs and side cabinet had to be measured within a quarter of an inch. It was in one of those tight-fitting chairs I sat, stacks of library books piled beside me, to begin my education in landscape design.

I had time and will and great interest in developing a beautiful garden. The Atlanta architect we chose believed as I did that a house should meet the specific needs of the individual family.

He and I were sitting on large stones just outside the entrance to the prefab discussing what I wanted in a house when he blurted out "Mrs. Power, do you realize what you have told me over and over is that you don't want a house. You want a garden!"

He was right. And his final design was a house with contours fading into our hillside garden, just as I wished. When the contract for the house was finally let, the fun began for me. I got oversized graph paper and began to plan the garden paths. These were made for convenience, but later they furnished border lines for bulbs scattered along in groups each spring.

So I laid it out. And bit by bit, day by day, year after year, I worked on it by sections. The sunny part was once a pony pasture; the shady part a grove of scrubby oaks. For three years I scattered dogwood seeds (all our dogwoods came from those seeds). I grubbed honeysuckle. I fought blackberries and poison ivy before the days of weed killers.

Far more has been planted than was included in the original plan. In forty years you add a thousand things: berries for birds, plants for year-round bloom, tree peonies, a raft of hollies, a fern collection, Japanese flowering cherries.

"What a beautiful place you have made of this, Darling," George said to me so many times as we shared a weekend lunch on our terrace, under the shade of the dogwoods.

### Two Tickets to Paradise

Some day this place
Will be our heaven.

"That's me you're kicking!
I'm down here looking
For the nodding trillium
From your grandfather's farm.
Why did you kick me?"

"Because you looked so kickable,
Running home to tell Mama Rabbit
About the ogre in the wood.

It is time you went on
About your gardening, woman,
Time you went on making
The most beautiful spot on earth,
Time I told you again that
I love you more than anything else on earth.

Are you tired of listening?
Two tickets to paradise, please.
You and your garden."

# Escuela Ecuestre

George came in briskly from the office on a beautiful December day and found me sitting in front of our new living room fireplace. He handed me a magazine. "This," he said, "is a new house and garden magazine to be circulated on the west coast only. We are placing some ads in it for a client. I thought you might enjoy seeing it even though it doesn't have any east coast circulation."

I found it a good magazine and was looking at the ads when something hit me. "This is it!" I said. "Just what we wanted for a different Christmas—a horseback riding school in Mexico."

"Tell me more," he said.

"I'm really serious. What could be more interesting than a horseback riding school in Mexico?"

A few days later, George came in with new information. "That's where Lucille and Jack are living," he said, handing me the ad, opened and marked.

We called these former friends and before we knew it, we were enrolled in a Mexican riding school in the town of San Miguel de Allende.

We began our trip with a clumsy mistake which taught us the value of keeping up with how the locals do things. George firmly believed railroads were the most dependable form of transportation worldwide. So we decided to travel by train from Mexico City to San Miguel.

Thus it was we found ourselves in an un-air-conditioned, wooden-seated car (could this be first class?). The car smelled like faint memories of a country hospital. We arrived at San Miguel de Allende at least three hours late.

We were taken in the riding school jeep to the escarpment which bordered the plain below the village. The riding school was a former ranch, with beautiful little cottages rambling down the hillside.

The school was operated under the direction of Harold Black, who had long been a horseman. He was so impressed by the jumping of the Mexican military riders at Madison Square Garden that he worked his way into ownership of this school in Mexico. George and I were probably his least trained riding students.

If we learned nothing else, we learned to be polite to our "betters" when we got our first glimpse of these beautiful riding school horses. Our first week passed much too rapidly. We returned numerous times over the years, always understanding that when the nine o'clock bell rang, we of the children's class were welcome in the big stable with the artificial horse.

We did learn a little about jumping and dressage. But we learned more about Mexico and how to enjoy its magnetic appeal.

## Vente, Miguel

  Tortillas are ready,
  Estímaulo senor,
  There's beef cooked with chiles,
  All you adore.
  Vente, querido,
  Eat well I implore.
  For mañana, quien sabe,
  There may be no more.

# Small in the Saddle

There were unmistakable sounds of horses snorting and excited human comments. Each one of us was setting out for high adventure. This was a staging area for a western horseback trip, a trip across mountains and alongside lakes; a trip so filled with beauty it would never fade from the memory of those lucky enough to be there.

Such a trip was not new to George and me. We had made them before and continued to make them until we were in our seventies, loving the warm days and cold nights, sometimes with freezing temperatures even in August.

On staging day our rancher-outfitter gave us a description of the new world we would be exploring, and we were assigned a horse to ride for the duration. The rancher who staged and outfitted this series of trips for the American Forestry Association had assigned horses according to descriptions he had been given of each of us.

I mounted the slow horse who theoretically suited a slow, gentle, old-lady rider, and both of us understood immediately that it wouldn't work. When Gerald, the outfitter, came by to check on us, I gave him a sad look and asked for another horse.

"Gosh, Mrs. Power, I don't really know what to

do. All the horses we've brought with us have been assigned. I'll just have to let you ride my personal horse."

Gerald turned away and reappeared leading a beautiful bay. There was only one problem. The horse was a giant, and I, his prospective rider, was five feet two. Nevertheless, it was love at first sight.

"What is his name, Gerald?"

"Kinda silly for a big fella, but I call him Papoose."

He led him beside a high rock so I could mount my huge new friend.

## The Wind Rivers

Down the Cliffside Trail
Scrunch of iron shoes
On rock. The slanting line
Of riders moves.
Faces pale with sunscreen
Daub. Hatted and booted
For the West.

But what are their
  thoughts,
Their non-mountain bred
  thoughts?
Down over switchbacks,
Horses bending to follow
The narrow trail.
These careful creatures,
Surely trust them when
  you turn,
Suspended over space,
  pretzeled
By your bent moving
  horse.

Don't look down
Count the wild flowers,
Name them. Blue bells
Sky-blue bells, foaming
  against rocks.
Spiky, magnificent
  paintbrush clumps,

Asters, elephant heads,
Tiny, glowing western
  sunflowers,
Bistort. (To know its name
Spells wild flower
  erudition)
And white columbine,
Flower of the dove
Master plan in flowers.
Heart touching, creamy
  explosion,
Cool, warm, delicate
  arabesque.

If, for once, your trusty
  steed
(Not completely trusted)
Fails to bend on a turn
Perhaps the pointed fir
  tops,
Green velvet spread a
  thousand feet below,
Will cushion rocks.

But you will have seen,
  absorbed,
Forever and forever
The shape and loveliness
  of
Incomparable columbine.

We'd been overnighting at a beautiful, small mountain lake for several days. George and I both loved fly fishing, especially where we could fish for trout. We had split bamboo fly rods.

This morning, as I pulled back the flap of our sleeping tent, I could see trout jumping. Even breakfast, our favorite meal of the day, didn't slow us down.

We set out with our fly rods, leaving horses behind. We would be fishing a remote lake not too often fished. In most areas there were restrictions about keeping your fish, a conservation measure. This lake was under no restrictions, however, because it was producing more fish than it could support. George and I wandered our separate ways.

I was exploring a little peninsula when I heard a yell from my husband, "Come join me, the fishing is great! First, let me pull this thing back upstream, then come aboard and we'll do some real fly fishing."

"This thing" was the bones of a large timber raft. It was built with a long boom to hold it on course. Rough board seats had been installed but there was no support to keep feet out of the water. George brought this awkward craft near shore and reached a hand for me to come aboard.

Then began the day of the trout fisherman's dream. The fish hit everything. When the day was done, we contrived a structure for our load of fish and carried it down the path at lake's edge. There was enough fish to feed forty people for dinner that night. And I have no idea how much was left over.

## Lac d'Argent

The club's dead now and the jeep track in,
Over rocks and through trimmed woods
That kept it private and remote
Has gone to brush.
Guides couldn't keep it going
Without money or management know-how.

Some who were there that day
Are dead now too, others ailing.
Yet still I see the shimmer and the gleam
Sometimes at night,
When sleep hangs back
And fretfulness and radiance contest the tossing hours.

Before breakfast, the men walk out.
"A perfect day, our last," they say.
"Ice round the lake but soon the sun
Will melt and burn away the mist."
We pour the yellow cream
On Dr. Jackson's Roman Meal,
Curl it over with maple syrup's smoky gold.
The cold air curls and curves with laughter, too,
And flaming logs crack counterpoint to start the day.

By noon, this lake is quiet glass.
Fish see shadows of our lines
And flip away with lazy tails,
Disdaining velvet-landed flies,
And we are bored.

"There's Lac d'Argent," says Claude, my guide.
"But it is far and quite a climb,
Then tous petit. Big trout live there
And it's not often fished."

So, lured, we go. "Portage, Portage."
Canoes upend and guides like beetles tote them on
    their heads.
We walk behind through woods as still as space.
By shadow-slanting time, we are weary and regret our
    choice.
"Courage," the guide sings out, "You see that hill? It's
    only over there."

And so, we come upon it.
The lake is still and stills the gauze of woven light
Through birches standing white and motionless
Along the shore. The stage is set.
Skilled paddles bend but do not break the quiet satin
    water.

Softly goes the line,
Mimicking peace
But hiding choking death.
My Royal Coachman, silky brown,
Touched off with clotted crimson,
Settles, rides the riffle.
Gentle as a breath.

Then silver breaks.
With rocket force the silence screams, shatters peace.
Broken shards strike chaos as the great fish leaps
In awful power toward his silver death.
"He missed, Madame," Claude says.
"He won't come back,
Not Grander. He is sage."
Claude sighs. The shadows of late day
Begin to curtain silver light
And we must stumble back to camp.

Long time has gone
But still at night sometimes
When sleep holds back,
I sink into the silver mist.
The great trout arcs in splendor,
Living still, and coming at my call
To bring me joy,
Who once to him
Offered careless death.

We were in an area noted for its wild flowers. Our morning's ride was up Tatoosh Butte, the highest spot in the area. There were no trees on the Butte.

As we came up the trail, we saw nature's masterpiece, the loveliest, most colorful expanse imaginable. Suddenly we were greeted by the sight of a painter, a man sitting at his easel, capturing the flowers of the meadow and the snow-flecked mountains beyond.

We rode over the butte until we found a place to tie our horses, then ate lunch among the flowers. As we returned to camp, I laid a trap for my darling.

The sleeping bags and other bulky baggage transported by the pack animals were dumped near the central campfire each evening. While we awaited our pack animals on this day, I explored. When they arrived, I picked up a sleeping bag. George was a bit suspicious. "You're not headed for that section way downstream, are you?" he asked. "That looks about one solid mile away from here."

"I have explored down there," I said. "It is the most beautiful spot in the west."

Have you ever bathed in a sunken bathroom, sitting on a sun-drenched boulder with a flowering orchid drooping over your shoulder? Have you known the joy of masses of blue lupine, Indian paintbrush, western sunflowers, fragile columbine, and a dozen other western beauties, with crystal water as your shower?

## Pretty Hollow Creek

Ah, come with me.
Watch the world fall away.
A mist dissolves and it is rain, silver rain.
Over the line of horsemen, over the giant trees.
Over the trillium and violets.
Over you on a silver horse.
And a gray squirrel barking,
Looking black in the silver rain.
Campers sit. The rain has stopped.
Fire glows in the quiet, green-black dark.
Crush, thump.
The Whippoorwill bird
Settles upon his great rock.
His call lonely, so lonely:
Whippoorwill, whippoorwill.
No world, no kind of world. Only you
And we, hearing the owls begin.
Drowsing by Pretty Hollow Creek,
Wrapped in thrilling loneliness.
We climb and the day is young
And there is a world, a fresh new world.
Long sun thrusts on the wild flowers
Breaking into glory where the stream pours down
And up into the balsam smell.
A veery's song mixes with our laughter.

# San Blas

We had been to the tip of Baja. There was a beautiful new resort hotel that flowed down the cliffside and dipped its feet into the eternally blue Pacific by way of a tropical garden, while the desert served as backdrop. The place was full of Hollywood name-people. It was dry and slick and smart.

When we flew into Mazatlan, we were ready for something different. We sat in our car in the airport parking lot for a while, looking at Mexican road maps.

"What do you think of the prospects of this place?" my husband asked, pointing. "It looks simple and hidden."

"Let's go," I urged, and we were on our way toward a tiny spot of the Mexican west coast we had never explored.

It was picturesque and primitive, a seaside village forgotten by time. There were stick huts made of tiny saplings stuck into the ground, and there were dirty, faded adobe houses with thatched roofs.

We drove around for a while, carefully watching out for pigs and chickens and potholes and children. The vegetation was tropical. Colorful wash hung drying on the line. The town seemed more Hollywood than Baja except for its unmistakable stamp of dirt, confusion, and colors, blended under the sizzling sun.

We found a small motel on the estuary of the river that bisected the town. It looked clean, smelled all right, and had a room for us. We booked in for one night.

Experience teaches you to expect the unexpected in Mexico. The sun dipped down just as we walked to the dining building, the last rays of light catching the color of the spectacular bougainvillea, a smother of radiant rose almost covering the building.

Next morning we asked about a beach. The motel had been placed on the swampy estuary a mile or so away from the ocean for protection against storms. We walked a dim once-paved trail until we came upon ebony sand with Pacific rollers breaking white and foamy as far as our eyes could see. We walked for hours, our only company birds. It was ours alone. We decided to spend more than one night in San Blas.

Next day we visited the old customs house which had been a busy spot in the fifteen and sixteen hundreds when San Blas was the take-off point for Spanish ships headed for upper California. At noon, to the beach again; our beach. You know the feeling if you have ever happened upon an idyllic and deserted spot.

Next morning we took the jungle tour. The tropical river was densely dim, and hot, and still, except for gentle waves against our boat. We stopped at a pineapple plantation. The owner's house was like a primitive dream. Then to a coconut plantation, where trees were hung with orchids.

San Blas waited four hundred years for us to come. Then it became our treasured moment in time.

## Reading Before Supper

There are words
To say everything.
Silver words
Which float away in dinging.
Spotted words
That flow and draw.
And words of gutta-percha,
Of life and living in the sewers.
Words picture what we do and are,
Faint echoes of our toil and sweat,
Our flying and stumbling,
Our sweet content
When red flowers turn to find last sun.

# Emma and Miguel

We were looking for a place to overnight in the small northeastern Mexican town of Linares. According to the guidebook we judged there would be a fair hotel in this area.

Finally we spied a motel. Tired and travel-weary, we stopped, soon to find ourselves in a large room with a glowing fire. It was a haven for the night. After dinner we talked with our host, Mr. Flores. George and I told him we were looking for a couple to go back home with us as gardener and cook.

We passed a short, pleasant evening conversing, then spent the night in a unit that bore the imprint of American-type motels of an era long ago.

Next day we continued on to Mexico City, where our leads were less successful than our pleasure in the trip. We saw the delightful "Ballet Folklorica" at the Mexican Auditorium, the Palace of the Arts and Sciences. We explored Mexico's most fabulous city along the entire width of the "Paseo de la Reforma." We reveled in the museums.

But we did not find our dreamed-of gardener and cook and returned home alone. Remembering the kindness and friendliness of Mr. Flores, my husband phoned him and told him we were still looking. He said he knew a reliable couple who might be interested.

Two months later we were once again in Linares, where we were introduced to Emma and Miguel. They became part of our lives for many years.

My husband had Miguel taught to drive. He drove not only with deftness and precision, but with a deep sense of pride, believing that George's dark green Cadillac was the world's most beautiful car. Indeed, he called it "El Flamante."

Once as George and I returned from a long trip to visit the beautiful gardens of Japan, we exited the airport terminal just in time to see "El Flamante" swing grandly up to the curb. In the front seat were their majesties Emma and Miguel; in the back seat, sitting ramrod straight, were Hector and Hero, the family Dalmatians.

It was a lovely welcome home.

# Sticky Yellow Pollen

Mother retired at age seventy from her position as French teacher at North Avenue Presbyterian School. Retirement for Mother seemed to be retirement from meaningful living. I had looked forward to having her join our household but my brother warned, "Sis, you will have to put her in an institution. She is getting senile fast."

Her self-sufficiency and valiant endeavors faded as she lost her edge on life. She clung to me and retreated from the world. It began to look as though he were right. Yet everything in me rebelled. Not our dear Mother, who worked so hard after Daddy's fatal accident to raise us. Not the unforgettable teacher remembered by generations of fifth graders.

The concerns expressed by a compelling new concept called "gerontology" hit home. I attended a panel discussion led by Dr. Ollie Randall from New York, an expert on aging. This aroused my interest and I began searching the stacks of the Chattanooga Public Library for more ideas.

I wondered if I would be able, at 70, to fit into a young society, or would I need contact with people my age who had danced the same tune?

And so, I devoted my time to discovering ways and means for starting a recreational center for older people. Ollie Randall started the National Council on Aging and I was asked to join when it was among the first nationwide citizens' groups devoted to aging.

Mother's attitude began to improve as we learned new ways of coping with our changing world. The day she decided to take a trip to Florida, where she taught school long before she was married, I shared her smile.

Mother renewed her girlhood love of painting and French and books. At age ninety-five, a year before she died, she attended the annual Senior Neighbors Christmas party.

### Sea of Daisies

Look back with love.
Look at the tall slim woman,
The noisy child at her side,
The sea of flowers that swirls around.

"Do you really love them so much?
Where did you learn about daisies?"

"Don't you remember, Mother, in my book,
When the children go to sea in a basket?
And the sea is a meadow of daisies.
Don't you remember?"

"I'll remember that you got
Sticky, yellow pollen all over your new dress."

# Sitting on Good News

Ruth Thompson and I got our local Senior Neighbors group started in borrowed quarters during the 1950's and it was chartered as a tax-free public service organization in 1960.

We started with no background of funding. Cartter Lupton was a great friend to Chattanoogans with needs. But he was retiring and modest about what he did. His nickname among agencies was "Mr. Anonymous."

One Sunday afternoon as I opened my front door I heard the phone ringing. I dashed in to answer and this is what I heard: "Hello, Ginny, this is Cartter Lupton. I have just been watching the program on which you and Mrs. Thompson appeared. You said your greatest need at the center is for a paid director. I'd like to fund this person for one year. Within a year your organization should show whether the need is real. I will send you a check, but please do not discuss the source of this income with anyone. The check will be issued under another name."

My reaction was so intense I hung up the phone laughing and crying. I called Ruth Thompson immediately, and we were off.

By this time we had a building of our own, through the assistance of the Siskin organization. It had been a railroad freight station, and our volunteers made hundreds of pleas to friends, manufacturers, labor groups, and civic clubs for materials and skills to refurbish and remodel it.

I remember gifts such as the beautiful flowered cretonne material given by Houston Jewell of the Chickamauga Bleachery for curtaining the seventeen windows of our big new recreation room. I remember visiting the building with John Crimmins as a young volunteer burst forth with her hopes for the future: "Do you know what I see in this old ticket-selling entrance hall? I see carpeting on the floor and crystal chandeliers!"

After nine visits to a carpet distributor, my friend Sue Ferguson got the carpet. Our screams of joy could probably be heard across the street at City Hall when we opened newly arrived boxes and found two crystal chandeliers. The electrical union furnished Saturday labor free. Gilman's gave us paint for the building, and members of the Painters' Union applied it on Saturdays, free. Siskin's had their metal-working and carpentry specialists there. Sue Ferguson and I took lunch on Saturdays for the volunteer crews.

Everything, every single thing we had in our original building was donated. Jim Franklin was the young architect who donated the plans and blueprints. Our portable meals service was made possible because we were given a stove, dishwasher, and other kitchen essentials by Billy Reece Samuel from her father's factory.

One humorous story. For a year or more remodeling of one large space in the building was complete except for the floor. Try as we might, we could not get that floor done. Finally one day I called George Wallace, my idea of Mr. Expert on floors. An unbelievably mismatched stack of floor tile was left over from the other floors.

George looked the situation over. "I can make it look pretty good, Ginny. And I'll do it next Saturday, but with one stipulation—I do not want one single female woman there to tell me how to do it."

When we went in on Monday after the Great Tile Laying Day, there it was! George had made a rather bizarre but perfectly respectable floor for what later became the garden room. And Louise Thomas helped us furnish it with gorgeous wicker chairs from her big sun porch on Lookout Mountain.

# Lloyd George May Have Sat Here

Senior Neighbors' first year was nearing its end. We were sitting in a nicely refashioned building, with many classrooms and a big recreation hall where we served lunch five days a week. Our cook had retired from one of the city's leading gourmet families, and she furnished mouth-watering dishes for our Senior Neighbors' luncheon menu.

I had completed my year as President of the Senior Neighbors' Board of Directors and was working on a program for the final meeting of the year. But I was feeling glum. Among our hundreds of gifts, there had been no banquet table and chairs which we could use. I was forced to visualize a group of our leading citizens sitting on wooden boxes with three or four bridge tables lined up as the council table.

At that moment the door burst open, and our young architect Jim Franklin swept in with a flourish, announcing as he came through the door, "You wanted a banquet table and chairs, and I've got them!"

"Oh, Jim, your words are music. Who is giving them to us?"

Jim hesitated. "Well, actually, my mother is giving them. When the Franklin architectural firm took over the Ochs mansion on old West Fifth Street, wonderful rococo furniture had been left in the dining room. It is trimmed with lion legs and heads. The story we heard was that while Lloyd George was British Prime Minister, he had furniture like this which Adolf Ochs greatly admired. Lloyd George assured Mr. Ochs he could get a duplicate set of furniture for him. So now you don't have to worry about your board meeting. If you still want the furniture, all you have to do is call my mother, and she will have it delivered tomorrow."

I headed for the phone, but Jim continued, "One thing I know though. If Lloyd George ever sat on those chairs, it wasn't for long. Those solid wooden seats are murder after a while."

"Maybe they had cushions," I said, and immediately visualized red velvet with long gold tassels at each corner. All we needed was a retired upholsterer to join our Senior Neighbors' group!

But that could wait. I was getting together material for my president's Annual Report. I was struggling with how to shorten it and still give credit for the overwhelming volume of gifts we had received. We had placed small donor-recognition plaques along the walls of the recreation room. When we counted them, we found we had 250 different donors.

I finished my report about an hour before the meeting. Then I opened the boardroom door and took a last look inside. It was practically regal in all its Victorian glow. The living room drapes from a board member's home had faded just enough to bring out the soft gold color of the walls. I had brought a bowl of flowers from our garden.

The Board meeting got under way with enthusiasm. Nearly everyone had been busy; most had accomplishments to tell. I proposed keeping the meeting to one hour. But well before that, people began to leave, pleading business or other engagements. When the time came for my annual report to be read, only a small segment remained.

"I'll try to keep this to ten minutes," I said. "But I believe it is customary to present the President's summary of the year's accomplishments."

My friend and tennis partner, Ruth Overmyer, stood up. "Just skip it," she said. "We all know what's in it. But if I sit in this chair another ten minutes, I won't be able to move."

So ended Senior Neighbors' first year of service to the elderly. Almost a half century later, it is still recognized as a leading Senior Center.

# The Keen Edge of Health

*Swinging and swooping,*
*Our wheels we guide;*
*Peddling along by the riverside.*
*Did we frighten you little bird?*
*It's only our exercise class you heard.*

For twenty years and more if you opened the door of the Senior Neighbors' exercise room, the sound of verse like this totally non-immortal poetry might have reached you through a sea of well-developed female legs. Bicycling on your shoulders with legs in mid-air is not one of the easiest exercises to do. The poetry cheered us on.

We sometimes referred to ourselves as an exercise-literature-philosophy class. It was one for all, and all for one, and we were developing close friendships along with physical stamina. A number of exercisers gave the class top priority for two mornings a week. Although it was purely voluntary, many remained participants for years.

Exercise and the outdoors have always been my thing. I well remember the meeting in the Methodist Old Stone Church, with Lup Patten officiating. His mother gave land at 100 Douglas Street for a tennis club. Other particulars were left to the discretion of our group of young players.

Our original little club house featured automatic hot water in the showers (then a rather new luxury), and a huge mountain stone fireplace for enjoying our after-game Cokes when fall weather was cooling.

The courts and first building for the Chattanooga Tennis Club were completed in the early thirties under the direction of two Patten brothers—Manker and Lup, who were excellent at promoting their sport. Tournaments soon began. We found a professional teacher, and were off.

For me, this attitude has persisted through life. When the National Senior games were established a few years ago, I endorsed them enthusiastically and entered qualifying rounds in tennis. I have been happy to win a number of gold first-place medals in the

game. It was impressive to see over 7,000 participants and visitors at the last tournament I attended. I would be happy to see 70,000 or 700,000 there, gaining strength and grace for life's final years.

# Joy and Peace

A garden club from Jacksonville, Florida, described to me as "a small group of garden friends" recently visited our garden. "Peace" and "Joy" were the words most frequently used in the beautiful notes I received from that group.

That is not an uncommon description for this garden where I am sitting in my thoughts; for I can ramble through its rough tree-lined paths in thought only these days. I can visualize my small pool, a grassy nook with maidenhair fern, water trickling over big stones, and clusters of brilliantly colored tulips against a woodland background completed with soft blue English bluebells.

I can see in mind's eye the "elephant pool" fish pond where my neighbor, Ann Boyd, once said she believed the huge pile of dirt nearby must have come from burying an elephant. It is ever thus in a garden. I love mine day in and day out.

And I especially love comments such as this one from one of the Jacksonville ladies: "I have seen most of the great gardens of the world, but none has given me the feeling of peace and joy I've found in yours."

George and I often speculated on the difference between a beautiful spot in nature, made by the hand of God alone, and what we call a garden.

A garden seems more like a landscape painting than a piece of natural countryside, even though, like ours, it may be a naturalistic garden. A Corot landscape with misty trees, a Van Gogh full of light and sharp angles, an early Dutch landscape with fat cows and fat trees—each has its own definite personality in arrangement, material, and something indefinable called style.

There are of course differences between painting with paint and painting with plants. No painter ever had to struggle with drought, ice storms, hurricanes, or a plague of snails.

My years of study taught me about unity, scale, proportion, and rhythm in garden design. But finally I found out that I never had anything at all to do with this garden, for it developed a personality of its own.

It does not sleep in winter as the books say gardens do. It breaks out everywhere, bare branches tossing impatiently in the wind; Christmas roses, wintersweet, and occasional camellias daring the cold.

While the forest floor is still brown, early jonquils, red emperor tulips, and blue grape hyacinths riot along the paths. Finally the whole glory of spring comes on with azaleas and blue scillas; depending on the weather, four to eight weeks of pure, wonderful color.

In summer the paths are green tunnels to unexpected nooks. Afternoon light slants through the trees and the noise of the water in the garden pools invites the dogs to jump in, while the late birds sing.

I have a delightful young god, Pan, set in his

own garden background. He replaces my Mayan ceramic girl who was smashed by hurricane Opal. There is also Ruth Thompson's baby Pan, glazed to resemble copper. He winters indoors and emerges with the spring.

Yes, my garden has enough to interest me every day I can live to see it. Hail, haven of joy and peace, I know you are there waiting.

## The Magic Wood

I look through the window in the rain
And see two wrought-iron thrones,
Shiny black, medallioned in gold
Their arms ending
In funny, gentle, golden goats.
Clean thrones, waiting expectantly
Against the trees, the soft, dark trees
That whisper in the rain.

In front, a grassy glade, small and lightly green
And a pool with lilies at the side.
A faceless king and queen come on
Clothed in floating mist.
They sigh and settle on their thrones,
Relaxed and happy. Then the queen
Touches her husband's shoulder and they laugh
Together in the rain.

The glade begins to fill with noise and stir.
From the wood children come,
Running and calling and playing in the grass.
They are happy children
Who never did get born.
Among the trees
High, trilling birdsong flows,
From throats of songbirds eaten by the cat.

Two dogs walk by,
Both polka-dotted black on white.
Hero sits beside the king
And gazes with appropriate royal splendor
Into space. But Hector sits,
Reluctantly, beside the queen,
Seems not to care for sitting and his eyes
Are seeking rabbits.

Rabbits come and make a circle
Play and eat petunias
By the big dog's nose
But he cannot see them for they are still alive.
"Hector hasn't changed," sighs queen
And pats his handsome, empty head.
It is a lovely afternoon,
Lovely in the rain, with nobody getting wet.

The children find a turtle in his shell
And bring it to the king.
He tells them science facts.
They sit to hear. And one small boy
Has white, white Irish skin, the queen is glad to see.
The cat that ate the birds
Jumps on her lap looking
Beautiful and gray and harmless.

She strokes the cat,
Hector stays quite still.
I know what queen is thinking:
That once when we were new,
And when the wood hardly deserved the name,
Was only trees and scrubby ones at that,
Growing on a hill; no dogwood, no azaleas,
No ferns to soften stones,
No paths that called to follow.

Much less to magic just ahead.

The wood was scratches,
Pencil scratches on a sheet,
And there was only now.
And now was nothing special
Rather plain and bleak.

The old nurseryman grew
Everything, but never praised,
Never said his plants brought magic.
Once he tried himself and wrote,
"Cavalier, my favorite."
And later in the wood,
Three giant azaleas
Lit the spring with ruffled fire.

Why do they burn with beauty in the wood today
When they have long been dead?

# Love Story

"How would you like a sample of the old maestro's best martini?"

"Wonderful," I said. "I've just been waiting for you and Hero to get back from that crazy three-mile winter's day walk."

"We both enjoyed it," Walsie said, "although the weather may have been better designed for Dalmatian than for man."

My husband gave me a light hug as he turned away from the glowing living room fire and disappeared in the direction of the kitchen. Hero, ever his master's dog, followed dutifully behind him.

I sat and dreamed in my chair beside the fire, watching the flames leap up the chimney, thinking of love.

In a few minutes a small procession came into my fireplace square. First, Walsie, my husband. He was carrying a small silver tray loaded with two martinis in the extra-small martini glasses we had found to prevent ourselves from taking too much alcohol. The martinis were frosted over and cold from the freezer. With them was a small plate of Judy Power's old-fashioned cheese straws, hot and red peppery.

Hero followed, and settled on his warm hearth

rug. George and I treasured discreet sips of our drinks. The fire burned low. We said not a word. But after a while, arm in arm, we progressed down the hall.

We passed the kitchen door. Immediately a firm but restrained "woof" was heard. This meant "Feed me now, otherwise, it will be eight o'clock, and I will be starving." I went in and fed our friend. He sat without moving, until a snap of my fingers gave him the signal to eat.

From our bedroom, I realized the sound of eating had stopped. Then he lay down outside our bedroom door, but never entered the room, although the door was open.

If you think this description concerns a dog rather than a lifetime love affair between a man and a woman, you are right. It is possible to follow the love and affection of a dog. But I cannot explain paradise.

## Night

Can diamonds break?
Can they drift in mist?
There is no moon,
But limning, lunar fog.
We see and do not see.
The world is clear,
And the world is vague.
Fifty years from now, in heaven,
We may recall this night
And surely, it will compare
Favorably.

## Photograph

There it was,
In the morning paper
We were dancing,
Looking into each others' eyes.
I could recall the music,
A misty, gauzy oldie.
We glided across the dance floor
Gently. Your hand was warm
On my shoulder.
I laid my cheek
Against the smooth perfection
Of your tuxedo's wool.
When I am dying,
Will I remember?
You are gone, but the answer
Is clear,
My darling.

# Tailored to Fit

It seems that mellow thoughts of old age come best while sitting bolt upright on pearl gray fabric-like plastic upholstery. When my sixtieth birthday had come round, my husband had quite recklessly offered to give me any automobile I wanted. "That Queen Mary's Electric Brougham you have been driving for twenty long years is going to fall apart with you some day. Go find yourself a new automobile," he'd said.

I'd selected a platinum gray Lincoln Continental with a black top. The reason for my choice was its enormous trunk. It was just right to haul manure and peat moss. And it had a front seat on which I could bend my knees normally and sit up straight while driving.

Hero found the back seat to his taste. As we progressed from grocery store to bank to seed store and all about town, I'm sure people considered the straight-sitting two of us a bit eccentric.

I have no apologies though. I've liked my life. It has been mainly lucky, with opportunities now and then to lend a hand. I've tasted sunshine often; ashes, sometimes. There has been the daily joy of living with mountains and flowers and cascading waters; and rarely, of glimpsing through mist the true-beating hearts of animals and men.

If a wheel chair should be my last chair to remember, I hope I can work out a few gadgets to make chair wheeling more interesting. And sitting there, I'll be eagerly watching for the fascinating dark curtains ahead to open.

Once I thought I saw it happen. I am not sure whether I was waking or dozing in my little dressing room rocker. But the curtains did part on a lighted stage.

At center front was a delightful little vehicle, a sort of individually-sized flying saucer bouncing lightly to and fro and appearing ready to go. I climbed inside and sat down in a seat that seemed tailored just for me. As I strapped myself in, I saw Hero was already there, sitting in his own back seat.

"Hero," I said, "I am so glad you are here."

"Of course I am here," Hero said. "You are going, aren't you?"

"Oh, Hero," I said, "you can talk."

"I always could," he said. "But you used to have trouble understanding me."

I didn't see a radio, but I heard the announcer. "For your listening pleasure, we bring you now a recently completed concerto by Wolfgang Amadeus Mozart with Rudolf Serkin at the piano, and the composer conducting."

The music started as our ship moved out. It was the most beautiful Mozart I had ever heard, better than any of my old favorites. I put my hand outside. A filmy phosphorescence trailed up from the stream of stars around us. Serkin's musical pearls danced on the waves and it was hard to distinguish sound from sight.

By the time the concerto was finished, we had reached the rendezvous point. The big command ship was there and Colonel Walsie was standing at an open porthole.

"Oh, there you are at last, Lieutenant," he said. "Good show. Glad you brought your friend. Are you making him comfortable?"

"I'm very comfortable, thank you Sir," Hero said. "There is even room for me to lie down frog-style on the cool floor, if my stomach should become too warm."

The Colonel looked at me. "You knew we wouldn't go without you," he said softly. "And now, if we are all here, shall we just get started?"

## Picture Postcard

       Every day I see Sandy Cay
       I see it in my dreams
       See it on my dressing table
       Among perfumes and creams

       See it as we sit on deck
       While others swim and play
       You touch my hand
       We're young again
       Part of the sea and spray.

## Home Again

Mrs. Williams' fishing hotel in Homasassa, Florida, is an unusual institution. Some of the older men in Chattanooga helped Mrs. Williams start it after the untimely death of her husband. The food is unreal—the cream is yellow, the vegetables fresh, and of course the fish are freshly caught. Pollack and Gertrude and Henry and Charlotte and George and I love the late fall fishing.

Sleeping quarters for guests are clustered in the big house. Being young and enthusiastic, however, we prefer the Cottage. Its decor is "submerged Victorian." There is a large open stove for warmth. But the most cherished decorative touch is the walls, solid with framed pictures, including our favorite portrait of a bulldog smoking a pipe.

Our evenings are brief in this delightful non-luxurious spot. We want to get to bed and be ready early for the spectacular fishing Homasassa affords if you get down there with the first sharp cold snap.

There is one difficulty. The bedroom that backs up to the living room fireplace has a heater, but the other two bedrooms are without heat. No time is lost in crawling into the chilly bed, pulling outing flannel pajama sleeves down around shaking wrists. We always draw straws for the room with heat.

George and I had the warm room last year, and we drew it again this year! As we collapsed into bed last night, I heard a muffled voice muttering, "Virginia Power, I hope you are satisfied." I smiled and drifted into a long, warm sleep.

This morning the air is much colder. We like to fish the first cold snap because it drives the seafish in for cover. For a short period of time, seafish and freshwater fish combine in the water. We go ashore frequently onto the cedar-covered small islands. We know there are rattlesnakes about, so we dress for protection in long flannels and jodhpurs.

I can hear the people in the unheated bedrooms chattering as they hurriedly dress, trying to get on enough outdoor clothes to get to breakfast. I'm cozy in my warm room, taking my time lacing my knee-high boots.

George steps out of our room and suddenly I hear giggles at the wide-open door. Fingers are pointing at me, so I look down. I am completely hatted and booted for the boat. My boots are carefully laced over my long johns, but I've forgotten to put on my jodhpurs!

They head on to breakfast, tossing a laughing promise back to me, "We'll try to save you a hotcake."

Visit the

# Wood-Wing Room

in historic
## Bulloch Hall
180 Bulloch Avenue
Roswell, Georgia 30075
T 770-992-1731

Copies of *Ginny's Chairs* are available

in the

Bulloch Hall Gift Shop

and in

bookstores everywhere

or contact

Phase II: Publications
5251-C Hwy 153, #255
Chattanooga, TN  37343
T 423-876-8456 F423-876-8457

or the

Virginia Wing Power Estate
PO Box 669
Chattanooga, TN 37401